A DRIVING GUIDE TO
SCENIC NEW ZEALAND

A DRIVING GUIDE TO
SCENIC NEW ZEALAND

Maps by Geographx
Text by Dave Chowdhury
Revised by Simon Henshaw

craig potton publishing

Revised edition first published in 2008 by Craig Potton Publishing
Reprinted 2010

Craig Potton Publishing
98 Vickerman Street, PO Box 555, Nelson, New Zealand
www.craigpotton.co.nz

Original text by Dave Chowdhury, revised 2008 by Simon Henshaw

© Text: Craig Potton Publishing
© Photos: Craig Potton and individual photographers
© Maps: Geographx

ISBN 978 1 877333 94 1

Printed by Tien Wah Press, Malaysia

Disclaimer: While all care has been taken to produce accurate information in this book, the publishers cannot accept responsibility for any errors and omissions that may occur.

Photographs by Craig Potton unless otherwise credited.

Photo previous page: Mt Ngauruhoe from Mt Tongariro, Tongariro National Park

Contents

Road near Lake Tekapo, Canterbury

About this guide

When I was a kid growing up in the 1960s and 70s our family would load up the car – a modest Cortina in the early years, and later the ubiquitous Antipodean Holden – for long summer holidays. Being recent immigrants from the UK and India, exploring our new home gave these holidays an added impetus. New Zealand isn't that big a place and the web of roads that criss-crossed the countryside gave us access to faraway places in relatively short order. These holidays took us from our home in Taranaki to Auckland and the Far North, Rotorua, Taupo, Hawkes Bay, Wellington, and occasionally to the South Island.

Back then roads weren't as good as they are now. I remember the terrible dusty unsealed winding roads between Napier and Taupo, through the Manawatu Gorge and in the Far North. Even some of the sealed routes were tortuous winding affairs through the North Island hinterland.

Since then, most of these roads have been sealed, straightened and no doubt made safer. The web of roads remains, the major difference is that there are more cars on the road than ever. That and the fact that tourism has become a major world industry, which has led to the development of a greatly expanded tourism infrastructure in New Zealand.

The other significant shift has been from the pre-arranged package tour of New Zealand to 'free and independent travel' holidays. Instead of plying the traditional tourist trade routes by bus, train or plane, tourists are travelling everywhere in hired campervans and rental vehicles or, increasingly, buying a car for the duration of their holiday, camping or staying in the many backpackers and homestays that have sprung up around the country.

This guide is a response to this trend in tourism. In it you will find descriptions of the major touring routes in New Zealand. Highlighted are the major places of interest, tourist facilities, travel times and distances, interesting side trips, walks, campgrounds, places where you might find a good coffee or a bite to eat. I won't claim it as being an exhaustive guide, more a greatest hits if you like. What this book is *not* is a guide to major destinations or accommodation – instead it is about the places and landscapes that lie in-between, to be used in conjunction with your Lonely Planet, Rough Guide or AA accommodation book.

Driving in New Zealand

Driver licences

All drivers must carry a current New Zealand and/or an international driver licence. Vehicles are right-hand drive and must be driven on the left-hand side of the road.

Safety belts

Wearing safety belts is compulsory for all occupants of a vehicle. Children under five must be restrained with an approved children's car restraint.

Speed limits

Speed limits in New Zealand are 100 km/h on the open road and 50 km/h in built-up areas. LSZ (Limited Speed Zones) means you must drive 50 km/h in adverse conditions (for instance poor weather) otherwise the 100 km/h limit applies. A range of limits applies at road works (30–50 km/h) and on the outskirts of urban areas (usually 70 km/h). If you're towing a trailer the limit is 80 km/h, and if driving a bus or truck it's 90 km/h.

Intersections

- Always use your indicators when turning (give three seconds warning before beginning the turn).
- Give way to all traffic not turning.
- Give way to all traffic crossing or approaching from your right.

Roundabouts

- Always turn left into a roundabout.
- Give way to all traffic on your right.
- Indicate when you are about to leave the intersection.

Traffic lights

North American drivers are advised that there is no free left turn on a red traffic light.

Rental vehicles

Tourists over 21 years with an appropriate licence can rent virtually any type of vehicle in New Zealand – from large campervans and all terrain four-wheel-drives to small two-door hatchbacks. Prices are variable and you tend to get what you pay for. Thus at the cheaper end of the range (between $30–$40 a day, unlimited mileage) you're likely to get a vehicle which is underpowered (1500 cc or less) and unlikely to have a good or functioning stereo system – considerations if you're planning a long trip and if there's more than two of you. Choose a rental company that offers Automobile Association breakdown assistance. Hirers are responsible for maintaining oil and water levels, but if your vehicle burns oil, keep the receipts and ask to be reimbursed as it's the company's responsibility to provide you with a well-maintained vehicle. Insurance cover is usually provided, but can involve some hefty excesses ($750–$1500). Insurance won't cover broken windscreens in some cases. There are also insurance issues around unsealed roads – see next section.

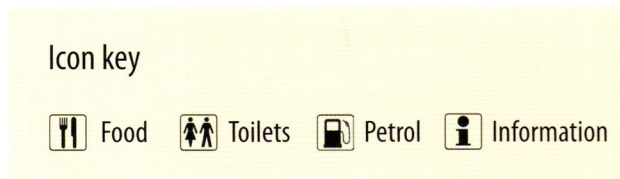

Icon key

🍴 Food   🚻 Toilets   ⛽ Petrol   ℹ Information

Unsealed roads

Some routes described in this book have sections of unsealed road. For the most part these roads are well-graded and maintained, and present few difficulties when driven cautiously. New Zealanders drive these roads confidently, sometimes too confidently. But for the overseas tourists used to paved highways, gravel roads can present a serious hazard.

In one accident I came across while researching this book, two German tourists put their car 50 metres down a bank above Lake Waikaremoana, having braked too hard on a corner and skidded off the road. Their vehicle stopped just metres above the water – they were extremely lucky. Unfortunately, accidents involving tourists on gravel roads are commonplace.

The best advice is to drive unsealed roads slowly – you're on holiday after all! Driving slowly gives you more control and allows a greater margin for reacting to other more confident drivers and irresponsible local drivers travelling too fast for the conditions. If you're driving an automatic, always select second or low gear to give yourself a measure of control on corners and lessen your reliance on braking.

Secondly, if you're in a rental vehicle, check the fine print of your rental agreement because some companies don't insure drivers on an unsealed road, while others exclude particular roads such as any road north of Coromandel township, Ninety Mile Beach, the last few kilometres to Cape Reinga, any mountain or skifield access road and the Skippers Gorge near Queenstown. The rental company argument that unsealed roads would be sealed if they were popular is misplaced when it comes to, for example, the last few kilometres of SH 1 to Cape Reinga. If this is an issue, renegotiate the insurance agreement, or find another rental company.

Slow drivers

I thoroughly recommend slow driving, but having said that, slow drivers on New Zealand roads are a particular source of frustration for following motorists, especially on hilly or winding terrain where overtaking opportunities are limited. Campervan drivers need to be aware of this. Convenient as these vehicles are, they are also slow, cumbersome and belch smelly diesel fumes, which is annoying to anyone behind. The simple rule for the sightseeing driver is to pull over at every opportunity to let others pass – it's such an easy and courteous thing to do.

Fuel

Petrol and diesel are widely available, but prices vary, wildly in some cases, the further you get away from main centres or routes, or when OPEC alters production, in which case rapid falls and rises in price come with little warning. In some areas the price of fuel amounts to daylight robbery, particularly in the Far North and the South Island West Coast. My advice is to fill up at the major towns and cities where fuel is usually cheaper than the smaller localities in-between.

Visitor information centres, cafés and toilets

One of the greatest improvements for both tourists from overseas and New Zealand travellers has been the establishment of an excellent network of visitor information centres. These will be found at all major centres and tourist destinations, usually well signposted from the main roads.

Another step forward has been the rising standard of cafés outside of the cities. While food is generally more healthy and appetising these days, many cafés confirmed that ownership of an espresso machine doesn't guarantee competency in its use. The cafés mentioned in this book are those with menus featuring more than the standard muffins, pies, paninis and plastic-wrapped sandwiches. Rather, they've made an effort to present more adventurous and creative fare, perhaps combined with art displays, garden seating or other interesting features. However, the quality of food (and my recommendation) can dive-bomb if there is a change of chef. You will find that most cafés close on Mondays and/or Tuesdays.

Public toilets will be found at or near most information centres, and in all towns, large or small. The cleanliness, however, is variable to say the least, which is a good excuse to stop at a café – café toilets are undoubtedly more pleasant.

Maori words commonly used in place names

awa – river or valley	puke – hill
hua – plenty	rae – cape
ika – fish	rangi – sky
inanga – whitebait	repo – swamp
iti – small	rere – waterfall
kai – food	roa – long
manga – stream or tributary	roto – lake
maunga – mountain	rua – two
moana – sea	tahuna – sand dunes, beach
motu – island	tapu – sacred or forbidden
niwa – rainbow	wai – water
nui – big	whanga – bay or inlet
pa – fortified village	whare – house
pari – cliff	whenua – land or country
pounamu – greenstone	

North Island Touring Routes

NORTH ISLAND TOURING ROUTES

29 TOURING ROUTE

Te Paki
3
Kaitaia
5
2 **4**
Kaikohe
Kerikeri
5
4
2 Whangarei
Dargaville
6
1
Wellsford
6
Helensville
1
Coromandel
Auckland
Whitianga
10 **10**
7
Thames
Pokeno
9
8 **7**
Paeroa
Waihi
Ngaruawahia
11
22 Tauranga
Hamilton
Matamata
22
Raglan
14
Te Awamutu
17
Tirau
Whakatane
25
Te Araroa
Ruatoria
Kawhia
14
15
11
23
24
Opotiki
25
Otorohanga
12
Tokoroa
Rotorua
Te Kuiti
Mangakino
Atiamuri
26
15
18
12
13
Murupara
Taumaranui
19
Taupo
27
Waikaremoana
Gisborne
New Plymouth
15
34
29
28
16
National Park
20
Turangi
36
Wairoa
31
32
20
Ohakune
34
30
Stratford
Raetihi
Waiouru
Napier
Hawera
21
34
Taihape
Hastings
32
35
37
Wanganui
33
35
Waipukurau
Bulls
Sanson
37
33
Woodville
Porangahau
Palmerston North
38
Levin
Castlepoint
33
Masterton
39 **39**
Martinborough
Wellington
Lake Ferry

South Island Touring Routes

SOUTH ISLAND TOURING ROUTES

46   **TOURING ROUTE**

WHANGAREI

DARGAVILLE

Ruawai

SH1 to Whangarei

Maungaturoto

(12)

Brynderwyn

Wairoa River

Kaiwaka

Port Albert

(1)

Kaipara Harbour

WELLSFORD

SH1 to Auckland

South Head

(16)

Snells Beach

Auckland–Dargaville
205 km • 4 hours

Auckland
▲
26 km
▼
Kumeu
▲
22 km
▼
Helensville ◀ 38 km ▶ South Head
▲
59 km
▼
Wellsford
▲
98 km
▼
Dargaville

HELENSVILLE

(16)

T a s m a n   S e a

Waimauku

(16)   Huapai
         Kumeu

Muruwai Beach

Waitemata Harbour

Te Henga Beach

NORTH

*WAITAKERE
RANGES*

Piha Beach

AUCKLAND

Karekare Beach

Northland

Northland is highly under-rated by international visitors who for the most part head south the minute they land in Auckland. This is a shame, because Northland's attractions – a combination of rich human history and extraordinary coastal and forest scenery – are such that it stands apart from many other regions. Much can be learned about early Maori and European social and cultural history, which is evident in the many marae, pa, colonial buildings and the historically significant Waitangi National Reserve in the Bay of Islands.

Drivers are well catered for by Northland's Twin Coast Discovery Highway route. Although the awkward title suggests a single continuous road, the 'highway' is in fact a combination of major and secondary roads (all sealed and in good order) that describe a circular journey around Northland from Auckland. The highway thus links the major west Auckland and Northland attractions: the Waitakere Range and west coast beaches at Piha, Bethells Beach and Muriwai; the kauri forests; Kaipara and Hokianga harbours; Cape Reinga; Doubtless Bay; the Bay of Islands and the sublime coastal resorts in the Waipu/Mangawhai/Warkworth areas.

The Discovery Highway is described here in three sections – Auckland to Kaitaia via the west coast, Kaitaia–Cape Reinga, and Auckland–Kaitaia via the east coast. SH 1, the major route north from Auckland, generally lacks the charms of the coastal routes though it is useful as quick access to different parts of Northland. For notes on SH 1 see the Eastern Section. Many tourists head straight up to the Bay of Islands and then cut west to Hokianga Harbour and Waipoua Forest via Kaikohe. However, if you have time, the complete circuit of Northland on the Discovery Highway route is well rewarded – up the west and down the east is my recommendation. Worth getting from visitor centres is the Department of Conservation pamphlet on Northland conservation camping areas.

1 Discovery Highway (Western Section) Auckland–Dargaville SH 16, 11, 19, 24

205 km, 4 hours

From central Auckland travel west on SH 16 (motorway) and exit at Waterview/ Great North Road, then follow SH 11, 19 and then 24 to Titirangi (good cafés here).

Waitakere Range – campgrounds, walks, swimming, surfing, fishing

The Discovery Highway offers fine views over Auckland as it wends its way along SH 24 (appropriately named 'Scenic Drive') through leafy Titirangi and up into the forested Waitakere Range. About 10 km from Titirangi is the Arataki Visitor Centre where you'll find information about the area's natural and human history, and the numerous coast and forest walks – get hold of the free Waitakere Ranges Regional Park brochure for information on these. The centre's balconies provide impressive views over the Waitakeres and across to the city. Ten kilometres from the centre is the turnoff to Piha, one of three impressive surf beaches accessed on this section from SH 24. The other beaches are Karekare Beach (made famous by *The Piano*) also reached from the Piha road, and Te Henga (Bethells Beach) reached from a turnoff down Te Henga Road near Waitakere village. Cafés on this section are located at the Piha Road junction and at Piha Beach. If you prefer your picnics without sand then part way along Scenic Drive is the Parkinson Lookout, which has a grassed area for picnics and a platform with views east to Rangitoto Island.

Kumeu/Muriwai Beach

SH 24 ends at Kumeu where the Discovery Highway rejoins SH 16. A little way south of Kumeu on SH 16 are several notable wine producers: Nobilos, Selaks and Coopers Creek, each offering cafés and winetasting. In Kumeu, Girasol Café at the north end of the town offers great travellers' food, while 2 km north of here is the more upmarket but very good Bees Online organic honey centre and café. Five kilometres north of Kumeu at Waimauku is the turnoff to Muriwai Beach (10 km) where the highlights are New Zealand's northernmost Australasian gannet colony, fur seals, a great coastal walkway, swimming and surfing.

Helensville

The Discovery Highway reaches the southern end of Kaipara Harbour at Helensville where you'll get good food (ranging from wholesome to wicked) and coffee at the Ginger Crunch Café. The Art Shop Café is another good eatery here. A worthwhile side journey is along the South Head Peninsula (45 minutes to South Head from Helensville on a sealed road) with fine views, swimming at Shelly Beach and Mosquito Bay, sea and freshwater fishing, hot pools at Parakai and the café at MacNut Farms Macadamia Farm (12 km from Helensville).

Kaipara Harbour

From Helensville the Discovery Highway (still on SH 16) follows the Kaipara River then turns inland and works around Kaipara Harbour. Several small reserves offer picnic sites and walks along the way. Omeru Reserve (signposted 18 km from Helensville) contains a Maori pa site, and a stand of tall totara and kauri; Port Albert is the site of a historic settlement on the edge of Kaipara Harbour 8 km from SH 16 (turn off 1.6 km north of Hoteo North). It's a pleasant, quiet spot for lunch, with camping and toilet facilities. A highpoint overlooking the harbour is reached before the descent towards Wellsford where the Discovery Highway links briefly with SH 1.

Kaiwaka

Kaiwaka is notable for its Northland regional information centre, and the unique Eutopia Organic Café.

Maungaturoto/Paparoa

North of Wellsford, turn west at Brynderwyn onto SH 12. The small town of Maungaturoto has Sugarbelles Café and a sign pointing to Piroa Falls. An 8-km diversion (half unsealed) and a 10-minute walk through a narrow tree-lined gorge, alongside a stream, will reveal a delightful waterfall – it's well worth visiting. A short distance beyond the next town, Paparoa (Sahara Café), another sign points to the Kauri Bushman's Memorial Park, which has a fine stand of kauri accessed by an easy track.

Matakohe

The famous Matakohe kauri museum is deservedly a major draw-card for this area. Here, in displays (including working displays of a mill and other equipment), exhibits and photographs, the story is told of the unrelenting logging of Northland's kauri forests through the nineteenth and early twentieth centuries. Allow at least a couple of hours here then drive away and marvel at how hard the pioneer loggers, millers, farmers and road builders had to work to create the landscape before you. You might then reflect on how little of the old forest remains, and be thankful that New Zealand's earliest conservationists succeeded in preserving any of Northland's forest at all.

Tane Mahuta, Waipoua Forest

Dargaville – campground

At Dargaville on the north bank of the wide and muddy Wairoa River the maritime museum is worth a visit, and an interesting local craft is hand-made paper at the Zizania Paper Mill and Shop. The Blah Blah Blah Café offers good food and coffee, but the choice eatery in the area is the Funky Fish Café at the magnificent Baylys Beach 15 km west of Dargaville (turn off SH 12, 4 km from the town centre). The Discovery Highway continues up SH 12, but SH 14 offers a quick (1 hour) route to Whangarei for those travelling east.

2 Dargaville–Kaitaia via Hokianga Harbour SH 12
183 km, 4 hours (see map overleaf)

This leg of the Discovery Highway is equal to anywhere on the South Island's West Coast. By the fastest route (via Kaikohe and SH 1), Dargaville to Kaitaia can be travelled in just over three hours, but there's little point in doing that. Allow a day, drive slowly, enjoy the walks at Trounson Kauri Park and Waipoua Forest, then catch the vehicle ferry from Rawene across Hokianga Harbour and follow the back roads to Ahipara and Kaitaia.

Trounson Kauri Park – campground, walks, picnicking

Trounson is down a well-marked side road off SH 12, 30 km north of Dargaville. (If coming from the north, an unsealed road to the park via Donnelly's Crossing leaves SH 12 about 6 km from the Waipoua Forest Visitor Centre). This large (573 ha) forest remnant contains some superb kauri, viewed from an easy 40-minute loop track suitable for all ages and even those in wheelchairs. Despite the cheesy poetry dressed up as natural history interpretation, one can learn much about kauri and other forest trees and wildlife on this walk. The Department of Conservation manages the area as a 'mainland island,' which involves intensive predator and weed control, so what you experience is a very healthy native forest and kiwi habitat compared with other forests in the region.

Waipoua Forest – campground, walks

Flanked by huge kauri, rata, kohekohe and other large trees, the almost 20-km drive through Waipoua Forest is the highlight of the western section of the Discovery Highway. The park was created in 1952, and its natural and social history are described at the visitor centre which arguably offers a more balanced view of Northland's logging and gumdigging past than other places. A lookout 3 km south of the centre offers a fine view, while a number of short or long walks get you right in amongst the ancient kauri trees, the oldest of which are calculated to be around 2000 years old. The two largest kauri, known as Tane Mahuta (Lord of the Forest) and Te Matua Ngahere (Father of the Forest), are the star attractions.

Hokianga Harbour

Continuing north, petrol can be bought at Waimamaku soon after Waipoua Forest, then Hokianga Harbour appears unexpectedly, beyond a rise with a view across the harbour to an enormous dune on its north bank. From here the road descends to the harbourside settlements of Omapere and Opononi. Families will enjoy Omapere's Amazing Maize Maze (open December–April), 5 minutes drive from the village off the road to the Waterfall Track; while the information centre at Opononi has good information about Hokianga attractions and history. Shortly after Oue, the Discovery Highway turns left off SH 12 and makes for Rawene (Kaikohe is a 45-minute drive on SH 12 for those who want to travel east to SH 1). At Rawene the ferry to Kohukohu ($14 for car and driver, and $2 per passenger) departs on the half-hour (from Kohukohu it leaves on the hour). A walk on Rawene's mangrove forest boardwalk, a bite to eat at the Boathouse Café or a stroll amongst the village's colonial buildings (Clendon House) are pleasant ways to pass time waiting for the ferry.

Kohukohu–Kaitaia
74 km

Kohukohu has a historic walk that takes in the village's colonial homes and buildings (the Waterline Café is recommended here). From Kohukohu the Discovery Highway takes you north along the edge of Hokianga Harbour before an enjoyable drive west through farmland and regenerating forest, past Broadwood and Herekino, towards Ahipara. In Ahipara, the Gumdiggers Café needs a few finishing touches but the food and coffee are fine. There is also an 18-hole golf course and access to the southern end of Ninety Mile Beach. Alternatively, you can drive east to SH 1 from Mohuiti to Mangamuka Bridge then turn north to Kaitaia.

Kaitaia

Kaitai is the winterless north's main commercial centre, with the visitor centre at the southern end of town. The Far North Regional Museum (near the visitor centre) is worth a visit for its displays of Maori history and artefacts and European exploration – especially the stories of Dalmation migrants who toiled as kauri gumdiggers during the late 1800s. Tours depart here for Ninety Mile Beach and Cape Reinga. There are no cafés worth mentioning.

■3 Kaitaia–Cape Reinga SH 1
116 km, 2.5 hours (see map overleaf)

The Discovery Highway reaches its northern point at Cape Reinga. The drive takes in pleasant Northland farmland for much of the way, crossing flats north of Kaitaia, and into more undulating grass-covered dunes and pine plantations further north with fine views over Parengarenga Harbour before Waitiki Landing.

Cape Reinga

Awanui

Big River Café (on the SH 1/SH 10 intersection) is a good breakfast or brunch option for those leaving Kaitaia early for the Cape or heading over to Doubtless Bay. At the northern end of Awanui, the Ancient Kauri Kingdom features a staircase built inside a giant kauri log, and crafts and furniture made from kauri wood that has been either recycled or recovered from swamps (all living kauri trees are now fully protected). There is also a café here.

Houhora Harbour – campground

Just south of Raio is a signposted turnoff to the Waggener Park campground, sited idyllically on the edge of Houhora Harbour. There's little to tempt taste buds at the café here, but the tidal inlet is stunning, and at low tide it is possible to walk across the adjacent streambed (though not across to Houhora Heads). For food, try the café bar at Pukenui, a little further north.

Waitiki Landing

After climbing to a high dune ridge with views of Parengarenga Harbour's inlets and mangrove forests, the road reaches Waitiki Landing where there is a store, petrol, accommodation and information.

Cape Reinga – walks, views

The last 21 km to Cape Reinga from Waitiki Landing should be driven with care as it is still unsealed and climbs and winds through regenerating scrublands and forests, and distinctive outcrops and cuttings of red volcanic rock. Shortly before the carpark at Cape Reinga is a turnoff to Tapotupotu Bay (picnic site and campground).

Cape Reinga, the lighthouse and views across extensive dunelands and remote clifflines are the main attractions at the road end. A 15-minute walk north leads to the lighthouse. The Cape is particularly significant in Maori spiritual belief as the

Cape Reinga

Te Paki

Spirits Bay

Waitiki Landing

Parengarenga Harbour

1

Houhora

Raio

Rangaunu Bay

Karikari Peninsula

Ninety Mile Beach

Doubtless Bay

Ahipara Bay

Awanui

SH10 to
Bay of Islands and Kawakawa

KAITAIA

SH1 to
Kawakawa

Ahipara

Broadwood

Mangamuka Bridge

Mohuiti

Herekino

Kohukohu

Rawene

12

Oue

SH12 to
Kaikohe

Opononi

Omapere

Waimamaku

Hokianga Harbour

"Tane Mahuta"

Waipoua Forest HQ

Donnellys
Crossing

Trounson
Kauri Park

Maunganui Bluff

NORTH

Dargaville–Kaitaia–Cape Reinga
299 km • 6.5 hours

Dargaville
▲
▼
54 km
Waipoua Forest
▲
▼
35 km
Opononi
▲
▼
94 km
Kaitaia
▲
▼
46 km
Houhora
▲
▼
49 km
Waitiki Landing
▲
▼
21 km
Cape Reinga

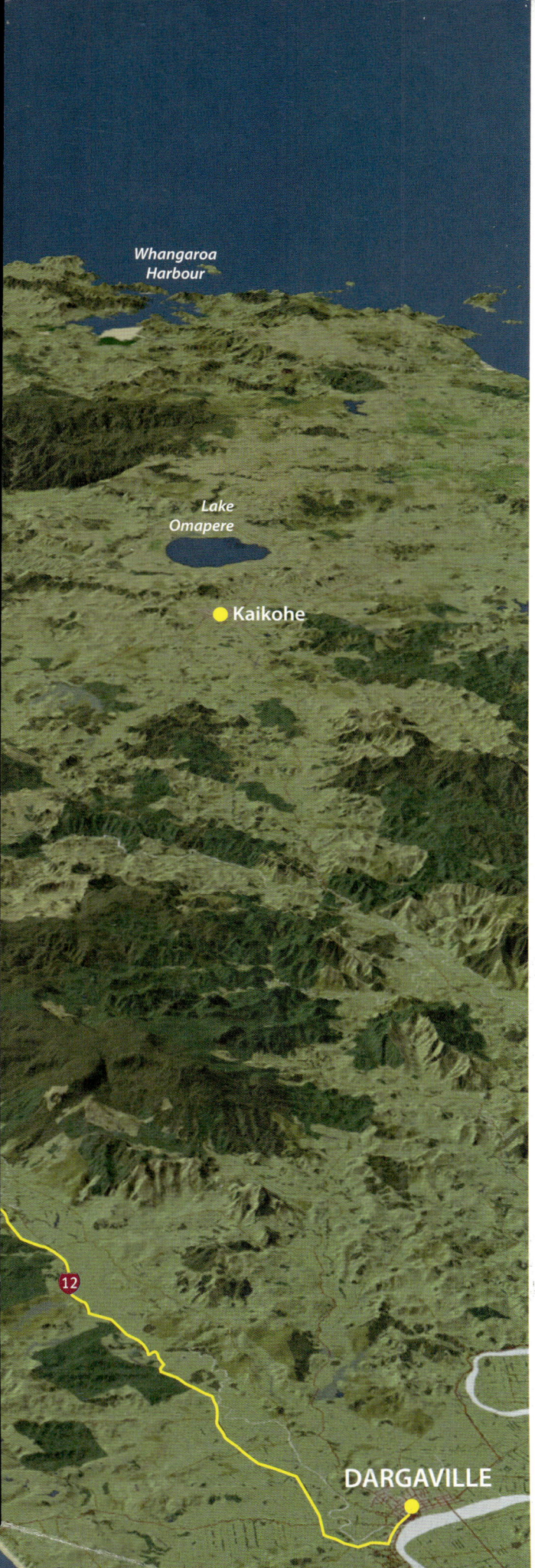

place where the spirits of their dead depart for Hawaiiki – the home of their ancestors. Eastwards on a fine day is a view toward North Cape while northwards the Tasman Sea and the Pacific Ocean crash together in foamy swells and lines of waves over the Columbia Bank. Below the carpark to the south is Te Werahi Beach and Cape Maria van Diemen.

Cape walks

A turnoff west at Te Paki (about 6 km from Waitiki Landing) down Te Paki Stream Road leads to stunning dune walks from the road end (picnic site) towards Ninety Mile Beach. You'll feel like you're crossing the Sahara Desert as you climb the giant dunes and gaze towards the Tasman Sea in the distance – so take some water. Similarly, a 30-minute dune walk from Te Werahi Gate leads to Te Werahi Beach and impressive coastal scenery in the vicinity of Cape Maria van Diemen. At Cape Reinga, walks lead to Te Werahi Beach and Tapotupotu Bay. Basic information on these walks (and the Te Paki Farm Park which encompasses much of the Cape Reinga area) can be found at the DoC depot at Te Paki.

Waitiki Landing–Spirits Bay

From Waitiki Landing a winding unsealed road through a Muriwhenua Incorporation forestry area leads to Spirits Bay where there is a DoC campground and wild beach. The drive offers excellent views of Parengarenga Harbour before the steep descent to Spirits Bay.

NB: Driving Ninety Mile Beach is not recommended for ordinary vehicles, and car rental companies usually prohibit their cars from being driven on this beach due to the risk of getting stuck in the sand and claimed by the incoming tide. Bus tours are the safest way to experience this stretch of coast.

4 Whangarei–Kaitaia SH 1
156 km, 3 hours (see map overleaf)

This is the quick route from Whangarei to Hokianga Harbour, the Bay of Islands and Kaitaia, however the road is often busier, and generally lacks the charms of the east and west coast drives. Petrol and other services are available at most centres. At Ohaeawai watch for the SH 1 turnoff or you will unwittingly end up on SH 12 to Kaikohe, which leads to the kauri forests and Dargaville. Further on, a turnoff at Mangamuka Bridge provides quick access to the northern Hokianga Harbour. Scenic highlights of the SH 1 route are the views across Puketi and Omahuta forests before Mangamuka Bridge, and the crossing of the hilly Mangamuka Gorge Scenic Reserve.

Karikari Peninsula

Doubtless Bay

Awanui

10

Taipa
Cable bay
Coopers Beach
Mangonui

KAITAIA

Victoria Valley

Totara North
Tauranga Bay

Whangaroa Harbour

Whangaroa
Mangamuka
Matauri Bay

Mangamuka Bridge
Kaeo

Takou Bay

1

Waipapa

Kerikeri

Lake Omapere

Ohaeawai
Puketona
10

SH12 to Dargaville

KAIKOHE

Pakaraka
Waitangi

Bay of Islands

Moerewa
Paihia
Russell

Opua
Okiato

11
Kawakawa

Parel

Ngaioto

Whangarei–Kaitaia
192 km • 3–4 hours

Whangarei
▲
22 km
▼
Whakapara ◄72 km► Russell
▲
48 km
▼
Paihia
▲
26 km
▼
Kerikeri
▲
23 km
▼
Kaeo
▲
34 km
▼
Mangonui
▲
39 km
▼
Kaitaia

Whangarur

1

Helena Bay

Whakapara

NORTH

1

WHANGAREI

5 Discovery Highway (Eastern Section)
Whangarei–Kaitaia via Bay of Islands and
Doubtless Bay SH 1, 11, 10

192 km, 3–4 hours

Northland's sublime east coast beaches and coastal resorts are in direct contrast with the forests, harbours and lesser-developed character of the west. The route described follows the Twin Coast Discovery Highway from Whangarei through the Bay of Islands and Doubtless Bay.

SH 1 (Whakapara)–Russell via Whangaruru Harbour (1 hour)

A highly recommended alternative route to Russell and Paihia is this scenic drive that takes in the eastern Bay of Islands' bays, inlets, forests and Whangaruru Harbour. Remote beaches and camping sites are a feature of the drive, with plenty of ways to fill in a day pottering down roads for rewarding walks and scenery. From Whakapara, turn right onto Old Russell Road towards Oakura. As you drop down the hill towards Helena Bay you will see signposted the surprisingly enjoyable Gallery and Café - a great combination of art and food with outdoor seating and garden to match. Continue on to Ngaiotonga. (The diversion southeast from Ngaiotonga to Whangaruru North Head – location of a popular campsite – is rewarded with a 90-minute return walk to the head for outstanding views.) From Ngaiotonga continue to the base of Cape Brett Peninsula. You can turn here to Rawhiti and the beginning of the Cape Brett Track. Otherwise follow the winding route past Parekura Bay to Russell.

Russell – campground, walks, swimming, fishing

As well as occupying a significant place in New Zealand's early European history, Russell is a major holiday spot and headquarters of the Bay of Islands' Maritime and Historical Park. A number of historic buildings and the Russell Museum are of note. Spot the musket-ball holes in the walls of Christ Church, and examine the Maori and British headstones in the cemetery. All the cafés here are very good, but Kamakura, Sally's and the Waterfront Café are all on The Strand and have the added feature of water views. For winery-café dining try Omata Estate, signposted along the road to Okiato. Drive or walk to the top of Flagstaff Hill for a 360-degree view of Russell and the Bay. Continue to Paihia on the ferry service to Opua (runs every 10 minutes from Okiato – see Opua/Paihia/Waitangi section below for timetable details).

Kawakawa

Kawakawa is 45 minutes from Whangarei. The main reason people stop at Kawakawa is to admire (and use!) the famous public toilet created for the town by the Austrian architect and artist Friedensreich Hundertwasser. Of the café options, Trainspotters in the town centre is recommended, otherwise there's Café Tuna on SH 1 at Moerewa just north of the town.

Opua/Paihia/Waitangi

Opua, about an hour from Whangarei, is reached by turning off SH 1 at Kawakawa onto SH 11. The main interest at Opua is the vehicle ferry to Russell which departs every 10 minutes between 6.50 a.m. and 9.50 p.m. in summer and until 8.45 p.m. in winter. The cost is $8 for a vehicle and $2 per person, payable on board. The coastal forest walk through Harrison Scenic Reserve (30 minutes) at Opua is highly recommended.

Paihia, 6 km from Opua, has several good cafés and places to swim or picnic. At the busy waterfront information centre you can organise sailing trips, bay cruises, fishing or dolphin- and whale-watching.

Waitangi National Reserve is one of the country's outstanding historic reserves. Here in 1840, New Zealand's founding document, the Treaty of Waitangi, was signed by Maori and the British Crown. Audiovisual presentations and historical displays at the reserve's visitor centre, and the *son et lumière* in the Whare Runanga (meeting house) are highlights of a visit here. Although the presentations skirt contemporary grievances against the treaty, and say little about how Maori were treated thereafter, they offer nonetheless a valuable introduction to New Zealand history. There is a café, and opportunity for walks in the Treaty Grounds and to nearby Haruru Falls.

From Waitangi many travellers cut west to the kauri forests via Ohaeawai and Kaikohe (allow a couple of hours to reach Hokianga Harbour – see Route 2). To continue north to Kerikeri head for the SH 10 junction at Puketona).

Kerikeri – campground, walks, picnicking

Kerikeri township (26 km from Waitangi) lies on the Kerikeri River in the Bay of Islands. Renowned for its Maori and European settler history, it is also a centre for crafts, culture and kiwifruit. Below the township in Kerikeri Basin is Kemp House, a former mission station built between 1821 and 1822, the oldest standing building in the country. Nearby is the Stone Store, a fine example of nineteenth-century stonemasonry completed in 1835, while on the hill behind Kemp House is the weatherboard St James Church, dating from 1878. Remains of the once heavily pallisaded Kororipo Pa can be reached by a short interpreted walk from the Stone Store. Opposite Kemp House is Rewa's village, a re-creation of an unfortified village that stood on the site in the nineteenth century. On the northern side of the bridge by Kemp House a walking track follows the bush-lined river for 45 minutes to the impressive 27-metre-high Rainbow Falls. Kerikeri has numerous eateries and bars but I recommend either Marsden Estate winery and café (on the road to Bay of Islands airport west of SH 1) or The Landing restaurant and bar down beside the Stone Store. Café Blue close to the SH 10 junction south of the town centre may still be good despite having changed its name and ownership. Makana Chocolates, close to Café Blue, makes fine hand-made chocolates.

Matauri Bay – campground, fishing

About 17 km from Kerikeri is the turnoff to Matauri Bay, a settlement populated by Nga Puhi who own and run the popular

WHANGAREI

Oakleigh

①

Marsden Point

Bream Head

Ruakaka

Bream Bay

Waipu

Waipu Cove

Langs Beach

SH12 to Dargaville

Brynderwyn

Mangawhai Heads

①

Mangawhai

Goat Island
Cape Rodney

WELLSFORD

SH16 to Helensville

Tawharanui Peninsula

Kaipara Harbour

WARKWORTH

①

Kawau Island

Waiwera

Hatfields Beach

Orewa

Whangaparaoa Peninsula

Hauraki Gulf

①

NORTH

Rangitoto Island

Motutapu Island

AUCKLAND

holiday park there. On the headland overlooking the bay is the striking memorial to the Rainbow Warrior – icon of New Zealand's anti-nuclear advocacy in the 1980s. The boat, bombed by French government agents in Auckland in 1986, now rests on the seabed off the Cavalli Islands northeast of here and is a magnet for scuba-divers. The short climb to the memorial by sculptor Chris Booth is a pilgrimage everyone should make. The views from the scenic drive between Matauri Bay and Whangaroa Harbour make it a worthwhile option for returning to SH 10 if you have time. Allow an hour to reach Whangaroa.

Kaeo – walking

Kaeo services the surrounding farming and horticultural area. Janit's Texas Diner, just north of the town, is styled after US 'roadhouses' and has a good reputation for those in need of steak, while its home-cooked cakes look a treat. Sixteen kilometres west of Kaeo is Puketi Forest which can be accessed from Waiare Road (turnoff south of Kaeo, unsealed). The Puketi Nature Trail involves a 1-hour loop through kauri/podocarp forest which also protects rare birds such as the kaka and kokako.

Whangaroa Harbour – campground, swimming, fishing

The scenic and sheltered Whangaroa Harbour is reached from a turnoff about 5 km from Kaeo. The harbour is surrounded by steep hills and volcanic plugs including the prominent St Paul on the skyline opposite Whangaroa above Totara North. The harbour is a deep-sea fishing base, and charter fishing trips are popular. Unfortunately a controversial marine farm has wrecked the view of the harbour on the drive to the settlement. Tauranga Bay east of the harbour has a great beach and campground.

Doubtless Bay – swimming, fishing

From Whangaroa Harbour the road climbs then descends to the pohutukawa-lined beaches of Doubtless Bay. The wharf at Mangonui remains a popular fishing spot, though locals claim (as they seem to everywhere, usually correctly) 'the fishing isn't as good as it was'. Mangonui's Waterfront Café and Gallery Restaurant and Bar offer two good eating options. Get a good fix of fish 'n' chips served in the traditional newspaper at the Mangonui Fish Shop, built on piles over the water with outdoor seating. Further along SH 10 is the sublime Coopers Beach, followed in quick succession by the beachside communities of Cable Bay and Taipa. Tokerau Beach (toilets) on the Karikari Peninsula is reached from an intersection about 8 km from Taipa. Also worth visiting on the peninsula is Matai Bay (unsealed for the last few kilometres, fine sheltered beaches and a great DoC campground), and Rangiputa at the mouth of Rangaunu Harbour – a wild and beautiful spot.

6 Auckland–Whangarei SH 1
173 km, 3 hours

Orewa/Hatfields Beach/Waiwera Springs

The first highlight on the route north from Auckland is Orewa, with a long sandy beach, ice creams and various shops. The best coffee option is the Emi Deli Café down Tamariki Avenue. Further north is Hatfields Beach, which is sandy but suffers from road noise. As you drop down over the next hill turn right for the large and popular Waiwera thermal springs with various pools and pampering services. Those in exploratory mood should drive out to the beaches of Whangaparaoa Peninsula. Shakespear Regional Park on the peninsula's eastern extremity is open to the public for walks and camping.

Warkworth

Boutique wineries, cafés, an art and craft trail, and numerous attractive beaches are features of the Warkworth area. A trip to Leigh and the Goat Island Marine Reserve (24 km) is one of the highlights – snorkelling and diving in the 'no fishing' reserve is often rewarded with remarkable encounters with large snapper and moki. The Sawmill Café, just out of Leigh towards the reserve, is an excellent establishment, while in Warkworth visit the Queen St Corner Café.

Waipu environs – campground, walks, swimming, fishing

Seekers of beaches and coastal scenery should leave SH 1 on a signposted scenic route 7 km after Wellsford (or alternatively and quicker, turnoff at Kaiwaka) and head for Mangawhai Heads, Langs Beach and Waipu Cove. The beaches are excellent and holidaymakers are well catered for. Recommended cafés in the area include The Smashed Pipi at Mangawhai, and the Naja Garden Café at Mangawhai Heads. The Mangawhai Cliffs Walkway from Mangawhai Heads is a recommended walk in this area. Return to SH 1 at Waipu.

For those interested in visiting New Zealand's sole oil refinery, the turnoff to Marsden Point is 21 km from a turnoff at Ruakaka.

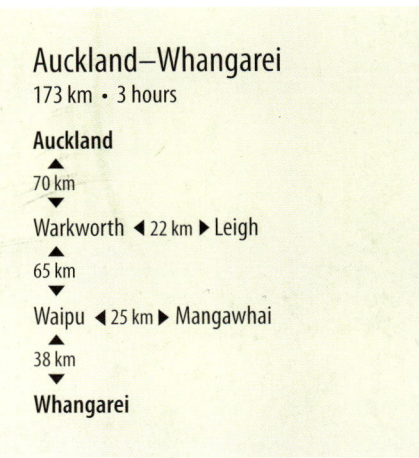

Auckland–Whangarei
173 km · 3 hours

Auckland
▲
70 km
▼
Warkworth ◄ 22 km ► Leigh
▲
65 km
▼
Waipu ◄ 25 km ► Mangawhai
▲
38 km
▼
Whangarei

Mt Karioi

HAMILTON

To Otorohanga SH 39

23

RAGLAN

Raglan Harbour
(Whaingaroa)

39

Ngaruawahia

Waingaro

1

Huntly

Rangiriri

Te Kauwhata

Meremere

Mercer

Waiuku

22

Waikato River

1

22

PUKEKOHE

Drury

Papakura

Manurewa

Papatoetoe

Manukau Harbour

Awhitu Peninsula

NORTH

AUCKLAND

7 Auckland–Hamilton SH 1
127 km, 1.5–2 hours

The drive to Hamilton down SH 1 involves one of the busiest stretches of road in New Zealand. Consequently, there's no shortage of places to refuel or find a meal at any of the centres en route. Huntly's coal mining museum is worth a visit. The SH 39 turnoff to Otorohanga (68 km to Otorohanga) is useful to note as it offers a bypass around Hamilton and access to Raglan and Kawhia harbours.

8 Auckland–Waiuku–Raglan via Pukekohe SH 22
158 km, 1.5–2 hours

This route to Raglan is more scenic and the roads are quieter than travel via SH 1 and Hamilton. To reach Pukekohe, leave the Auckland motorway at Drury and turn onto SH 22. The route then follows SH 22 until it meets SH 23, 14 km east of Raglan.

Waiuku/Awhitu Peninsula – campground, swimming, picnicking
Waiuku (28 km from Drury, 50 minutes from central Auckland), a charming rural town at the base of the Awhitu Peninsula on the edge of Manukau Harbour, is worth visiting for its historic buildings, pioneer museum and beaches and campgrounds on the peninsula. You can also visit the restored lighthouse at the northern end of the peninsula. Grab a copy of the Franklin Country Funmap for good local activities. Two cafés in Waiuku took my fancy: Rosli's Café and Café Alba. Karioitahi beach close to Waiuku has great views of the wild west coast, and recommended swimming beaches are at Orua Bay, Big Bay and Graham's Beach (but get local safety advice). Birdwatchers will be well rewarded at Awhitu Regional Park and along the tidal flats of Manukau Harbour. Stay at the very nice Castaways apartment-style accommodation and dine at Agave Restaurant (open Wed–Sun).

Bridal Veil Falls, Raglan

Pukekohe–Raglan
108 km, 1.5 hours

Pukekohe (50 km from Auckland) is a bustling town servicing the surrounding market gardening region. The drive to Raglan winds through undulating plains and hill country and occasional forest remnants including a fine stand of totara at St Albans near Waingaro. Natural hot springs at Waingaro have been developed into a public spa – a fun place for families, with an adjacent motorcamp and tavern. The last few kilometres to the SH 23 junction are unsealed.

Raglan – campground, walks, swimming, surfing, picnicking, fishing
Raglan is a justly popular holiday resort on the edge of Whaingaroa Harbour. Renowned (among other things) for its surf beaches, kite surfing, orca, and its stone symposium, the settlement has a laid back holiday feel, and its residents have made a strong commitment to turning their village into an environmentally friendly locale. There are several good cafés on the main street; try Tongue and Groove or Aqua Velvet. Walks to Mt Karioi from the coast (allow 4–5 hours) and the Bridal Veil Falls (20 minutes return) near Te Mata are popular, as is the Te Toto Gorge Track – these are described in a DoC brochure available at the Raglan visitor centre. The 50 km 'back route' to Kawhia along Raglan Road via Te Mata and Makomako is a recommended scenic drive, though half of it is unsealed and requires care, particularly on narrower sections at the Kawhia end. Allow an hour from Raglan to reach Hamilton along SH 23.

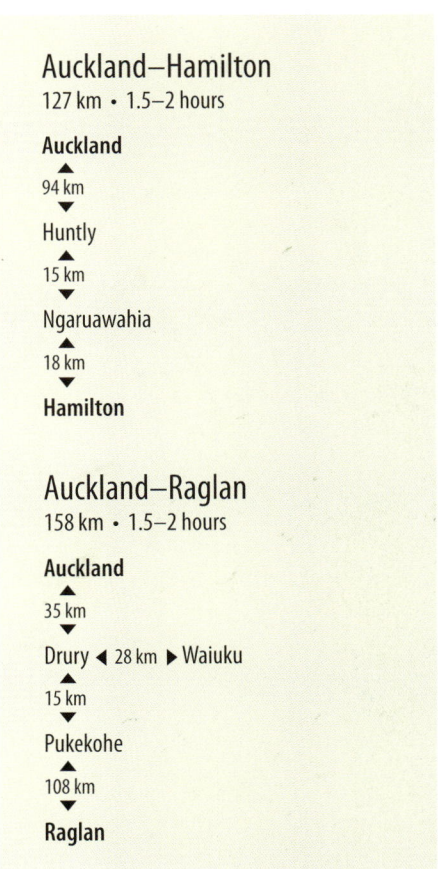

Auckland–Hamilton
127 km · 1.5–2 hours

Auckland
▲
94 km
▼
Huntly
▲
15 km
▼
Ngaruawahia
▲
18 km
▼
Hamilton

Auckland–Raglan
158 km · 1.5–2 hours

Auckland
▲
35 km
▼
Drury ◄ 28 km ► Waiuku
▲
15 km
▼
Pukekohe
▲
108 km
▼
Raglan

Waihou River
SH2 to Paeroa
SH27 to Matamata

Kopu
THAMES
25

Firth
of
Thames

Waitakaruru
25

Miranda

Maramarua

Kaiaua

Mangatawhiri

SH1
Hamilto

2

Matingarahi

HUNUA RANGES

Bombay

Orere

1

Kawakawa Bay

Drury

Papakura

Clevedon

Manurewa

Whitford

East Tamaki
Papatoetoe

Hauraki Gulf

Pakuranga

Manukau Harbour

1

NORTH

AUCKLAND

9 Auckland–Thames SH 1, 2, 25
115 km, 90 minutes

The quickest route from Auckland to Thames is via SH 1, 2 and 25 and takes 90 minutes on a good traffic-less day without delays at Kohu Bridge near Thames. If you take this route you have the option of cutting directly to Miranda (see below) by taking a turn left off SH 2 (signposted) just after Mangatawhiri.

The SH 25 turnoff to Thames via Waitakaruru is 35 km from the SH 1 exit on the Auckland–Hamilton Expressway. Mangatawhiri's Chateau Crème Delight sells great ice creams. The Black Beagle Café a kilometre past Maramarua is another potential place for a break.

Auckland–Thames
via Firth of Thames
125 km · 2 hours

Auckland
▲
29 km
▼
Papakura
▲
27 km
▼
Kawakawa Bay
▲
18 km
▼
Matingarahi
▲
21 km
▼
Miranda
▲
32 km
▼
Thames

Auckland–Thames via Pakuranga, Firth of Thames coast, SH 25
127 km, 2 hours

I'd recommend this slightly longer scenic drive to Thames from Pakuranga that skirts along the Firth of Thames and the base of the Hunua Range. Leave the SH 1 motorway south of Auckland by taking the southeastern SH 10 exit then following the signs to Pakuranga. Turn right into Ti Rakau Drive (SH 8) where you may spot the sign pointing to Whitford. SH 8 becomes SH 5. Turn left into Chapel Road (still SH 5) then watch for the right turn into Whitford Road. City becomes countryside at last! At Whitford turn right and follow signs toward Clevedon. Tell everyone in the cheap seats to behave themselves or you will drive straight past the Clevedon Chocolate Shop (stocked with a tempting variety of hand-made chocolates). A good lunch option is the Clevedon Café which offers more of a sit-down restaurant menu rather than lighter café fare.

At Kawakawa Bay (store, fuel) views spread north to Waiheke and Ponui Islands. The road climbs through the forests of Te Morehu Scenic Reserve to Orere and the Orere Point campground. The road narrows between Matingarahi and Kaiaua – whose fish and chip shop has twice been voted the best in New Zealand.

Miranda's Shorebird Centre is the first port of call for exploring the internationally important wading bird reserve in the firth's tidal shallows across the road, one of several locations in New Zealand where Northern Hemisphere migratory species congregate to escape the northern winter. There is walking access to the firth opposite the centre, and about 2 km further south (from a signposted rest area through land covenanted with the Queen Elizabeth II Trust) – at both places please respect the fact that you are crossing private land. Miranda's other attraction is its natural hot springs located at a holiday park/campground south of the shorebird centre.

Mongolian plover, Miranda

Colville

Port Jackson

MOEHAU RANGE

Colville

Kennedy Bay

Whangapoua Harbour

Kuaotun

Amodea Bay

Papaaroha

COROMANDEL

Coromandel Harbour

25

Waiau

WHITIAI

25

SH25
Wai

Manaia

C O R O M A N D E L   R A N G E

Kereta

Tapu River

NORTH

Tapu

25

Coromandel Peninsula (West)
108 km • 3 hours

Te Puru

Thames
▲
54 km
▼
Coromandel
▲
28 km
▼
Colville
▲
26 km
▼
Cape Colville

Firth of Thames

THAMES

Kauaeranga River

🔟 Coromandel Peninsula SH 25, 25a
Circuit 264 km

The Coromandel Peninsula is one of the North Island's top holiday destinations. Sheltered bays, beaches and harbours, the Coromandel Range, a thriving arts and crafts community and alternative lifestylers, and a long Maori and European history are among its attractions. Whilst the summer weather is usually good, Coromandel is prone to 'weather bombs' or just plain bad weather. Slips and road washouts are not uncommon, so it pays to contact information centres to check road conditions before setting out.

Thames–Coromandel SH 25
54 km, 1 hour

Thames – campground, walks

Thames' attractions include its museum (which recounts gold rush and logging eras) and the mineral displays at the mining school. Those interested in arts and crafts can purchase a guide to Coromandel's galleries at the Thames Information Centre. East of Thames in the Kauaeranga Valley (14 km) is a DoC visitor centre, a base for camping, walks and information about recreational activities in the Coromandel Range. A working kauri dam is a highlight. On Pollen Street the Sola Café make a simply smashing cup of coffee, while nearby Chequers Café appears to be the second-best option in town. A boardwalk through mangroves to a Forest and Bird Protection Society bird hide begins near the Goldfields shopping complex and model railway. The best time to observe birdlife from the hide is within 2 hours before or after high tide.

Coromandel

Lined with pohutukawa, the road up the Thames coast to Coromandel is a lovely drive past mangrove-fringed bays, beaches, small settlements and craft galleries. At Waiomu the Coast to Kauri track (allow up to 3 hours return, brochure available) offers an easy walk from the coast past mining relics and regenerating forest to a magnificent stand of kauri. At Tapu (19 km from Thames), the diversion to the Rapaura Watergardens (6.5 km along the Tapu–Coroglen Road) is highly recommended. From Kereta, the road to Coromandel climbs to points overlooking Manaia and Coromandel harbours and the Hauraki Gulf. Stalls selling fresh mussels and oysters are found as the road rounds flats on the edge of Coromandel Harbour.

Coromandel's charm lies in the atmosphere conjured by its numerous sidewalk cafés, galleries and historic buildings dating from the gold rushes of the 1850s and 60s. The mining school has working models of quartz-crushing machinery and other nineteenth-century mining relics. Gold was struck for the first time in New Zealand at Driving Creek, a few kilometres north of Coromandel. These days Driving Creek is a haven for artisans and location of the famous narrow-gauge Driving Creek railway.

Driving Creek also features potteries, working steam engines, a brickworks and café. Ten minutes past Driving Creek up Kennedy Bay Road (steep and unsealed) is the Tokatea Lookout and walk – a superb viewpoint. Café recommendations: Umu (for coffee, seafood and bad service), the Pepper Tree (better service but more expensive) and Driving Creek Café for its relaxed garden setting, vegetarian food and a delectable selection of cakes. Back in town, I was impressed with The Source, a cooperative venture featuring the work of nine Coromandel craft artists located on Coromandel's main street.

Colville

Thirty minutes (28 km) north of Coromandel is this friendly village that launched the region's reputation for alternative lifestyles. The Colville Caff is reason alone to visit. Before Colville there are serviced campgrounds at Shelly, Long and Amodeo bays and at Papaaroha. Legstretcher: The 40-minute coastal forest walk at Papaaroha.

Cape Colville – campground, walks

Many make the scenic drive north around the Moehau Range to Cape Colville/Port Jackson. However, the road is unsealed, narrow and winding, so allow 2 hours each way from Coromandel. There are DoC campgrounds at Fantail Bay (23 km from Colville) and at Fletcher Bay, five minutes from Port Jackson.

Coromandel–Whitianga SH 25
46 km, 1 hour

Allow 1 hour for the pleasant drive along SH 25 which crosses the Coromandel Range to Whangapoua Harbour and Kuaotunu settlement (petrol, dairy, pleasant beaches and a campground nearby). Then it's a 16-km drive through another fragment of Coromandel Forest Park to Mercury Bay and Whitianga.

Coromandel–Whitianga via the '309 Road'
32 km, 50 minutes

An unsealed scenic route across the Coromandel Range, which begins off SH 25 about 4 km south of Coromandel. Highly recommended by the locals, this is nonetheless a rather narrow and winding drive. Apart from forest scenery, the highlights are the Waiau Waterworks (an eccentric and fun garden and café) 9 km from Coromandel, Waiau Falls (popular swimming hole) and the nearby Kauri Grove (12 km), one of the few remaining unlogged kauri stands in the region: allow 20 minutes to walk through here on an easy path.

Port Jackson

Cape Colville

MOEHAU RANGE

Mercury Islands

Colville

Amodea Bay

Papaaroha

Kennedy Bay

Coromandel Harbour

COROMANDEL **25**

Whangapoua Harbour

Kuaotunu

Waiau

SH25 to Thames

Manaia

WHITIANGA

Mercury Bay

Cooks Beach

Hahei

COROMANDEL RANGE

25

Hot Water Beach

NORTH

Tairua

Pauanui

SH25A to Thames

Opoutere

Wharekawa Harbour

Onemana

25

Whitianga–Whangamata
81 km • 1.5 hours

Whitianga ◀ 32 km ▶ Coromandel via 309 Rd
▲
26 km
▼
Whenuakite
▲
31 km
▼
Hikuai ◀ 30 km ▶ Thames via Inland Rd
▲
24 km
▼
Whangamata

WHANGAMATA

Bay of Ple

Whitianga–Whangamata
81 km, 1.5 hours

Whitianga – campground, swimming, fishing
Once a major colonial port supporting the trade in kauri and kauri gum, Whitianga is now a rural service town and holiday resort. In summer tourists and holidaymakers gather to enjoy the area's beaches, water activities and coastal scenery. The best cafés are a little hidden away but worth seeking out: Café Nina on Victoria Street behind the library, and Coghill House Café down Coghill Street. You can take the passenger ferry ($2) for a quick crossing to Ferry Landing and walking access to Cooks Beach.

Hahei/Cooks Beach – campground, walks, swimming
These are two of the Whitianga area's most popular locations. Hahei is 37 km from Whitianga (turnoff at Whenuakite) and its attractions include its beach, the Te Whanganui-A-Hei Marine Reserve and the Cathedral Cove walkway – an excellent interpreted coastal walk (2 hours return) with spectacular scenery. Luna Café in the village makes great coffee. At Hot Water Beach, south of Hahei you can dig out your own natural spa on the beach two hours either side of low tide (hire a spade from nearby shops). Hot Water Beach also has the Hot Waves café in a nice garden setting.

To reach Cooks Beach turn left on Purangi Road 2 km from the Whenuakite intersection. Cooks Beach is another sublime safe swimming area, and where Captain Cook and his astronomer observed the transit of Mercury across the sun in 1769. The Shakespeare Cliff walk offers panoramic views of Mercury Bay. It's a short drive from here to Flaxmill Bay (Eggscentric Café) and Ferry Landing (Coro Café) opposite Whitianga.

Tairua/Pauanui – campground, walk, swimming
Tairua (37 km from Whitianga) is an idyllic settlement near the mouth of Tairua Harbour. Mount Paku dominates the harbour entrance, but fortunately you can drive most of the way up before climbing 178 steps and an easy rocky section to take you to a spectacular 360-degree view of land and sea. Out of the Blue Café has a good reputation, offering vegetarian food as well as meatier options.

Across the harbour (29 km by road via Hikuai), is the exclusive, purpose-built holiday town of Pauanui. There is a good surf beach here and a rewarding though steep climb up Pauanui Mountain from the south end of Pauanui beach. Due to almost non-existent signage you risk getting lost in this town, however, if you need a good cake fix the Chocolate Pretzel Café almost makes the risk worthwhile.

At Hikuai (fuel), 11 km from Tairua, you can return to Thames (30 km) via SH 25a, which wriggles through the Coromandel Range with excellent views of the Pinnacles along the way. Also at Hikuai is the turnoff to the Broken Hills and Puketui Valley for 1/2–2-hour bush walks exploring relics of the early mining

period. Take a torch as some tracks feature old (though safe) tunnels, including one that is 500 metres long.

Between Hikuai and Whangamata, side roads lead to Opoutere and Onemana beaches. Opoutere is halfway round mangrove-lined Wharekawa Harbour which has a great youth hostel and campground on its shores. Walks in dunelands and to the wildlife reserve (birdwatching) in the harbour estuary are recommended here. Onemana, more developed, has a lovely beach, views to the Alderman Islands, and Café Onemana.

Whangamata – campground, swimming
Whangamata's 3.8 km Ocean Beach has a renowned surf break. Like Whitianga, the population swells in summer and cafés and restaurants have emerged to meet the demand for good food and beverages. Try Rossini or Vibes cafés along the main street.

From Whangamata, SH 25 continues south for 29 km, past Whiritoa Beach to Waihi.

Waihi – campground, walks, swimming
Waihi is a modern goldmining town and holiday destination – try the Kava or Quartz cafés on busy Seddon Street, or the Ti-Tree Café on quieter Haszard Street. Waihi trades on its long mining history with historic walks, relics, museum and vintage railway. If you've never visited an opencast mine, this is the place. Waihi's 'heart of gold', the Martha Mine in the centre of the town, is open for tours, otherwise find the Moresby Ave lookout where interpretation panels would have you believe that ripping open a 300-metre deep hole is a most natural and environmentally sensitive activity.

Cathedral Cove, Coromandel Peninsula

KAINGAROA FOREST

Huka Falls

Aratiatia

Waikato River

Wairakei

TAUP

La
Tau

5

Golden Springs

1

SH38 to
Murupara

Waiōtapu

Waikato River

Atiamuri

SH30 t
Whakamar

Waimungu

5

KINLEITH FOREST

Kinleith

Whakarewarewa

ROTORUA

TOKOROA

SH3
Whakar

Lake
Rotorua

Ngongotaha

1

M A M A K U   P L A T E A U

Putaruru

5

1

Tapapa

Tirau

SH28,29 to
Tauranga

SH
Ham

SH24,29 to
Tauranga

27

Waihou River

MATAMATA

NORTH

11 Auckland–Rotorua SH 1, 2, 27, 5
241 km, 3.5 hours

The fastest route to Rotorua from Auckland is the route via SH 1, 2, 27 and 5. Travelling from Auckland down SH 1, turn onto SH 2 south of Bombay and follow it through Mangatawhiri and Maramarua to Mangatarata, where you take SH 27. In the small town of Waharoa (just north of Matamata) you will find the very interesting Kaimai Café serving breakfast and lunch, and producing a boutique range of tasty cheeses.

Matamata
The well-established Workmans Café on Matamata's main street is the best café between Auckland and Rotorua, closely followed by Eat directly opposite. Tours of Hobbiton village, built for Peter Jackson's film trilogy *The Lord Of The Rings*, is the town's most popular tourist activity these days. Book tours at the information centre, where you can also get directions for a worthwhile side trip to the Wairere Falls (45-minute walk one way).

Tirau
Tirau has a novel information centre and adjacent gallery promoting woolly things, and seemingly far too many good cafés for the small size of the town (try the Cabbage Tree or Alley Cats).

Just south of Tirau turn east onto SH 5 to Rotorua. From Tapapa SH 5 climbs onto the forested Mamaku Plateau — lovely driving through forest and volcanic landscapes to Ngongotaha on the shores of Lake Rotorua, 7 km from the Rotorua city centre.

12 Auckland–Taupo SH 2, 27, 1
277 km, 4 hours

Follow the route above to Tirau where SH 27 rejoins SH 1. From Tirau it's a straight run down SH 1 through Putaruru, the mill towns of Tokoroa and Kinleith and long avenues of pine plantations in Kinleith Forest. (Allow 40 minutes to reach Rotorua via SH 30, which intersects 19 km from Tokoroa.) In Putaruru stop at the tiny Over the Moon Dairy Company to taste-test their delicious cheeses (they make great coffee too). Tokoroa's Scoffers Café on Roseberry Street (one block from the information centre) is a foodie's oasis where you'll get good coffee as well. Roughly 15 km south of Atiamuri is the turnoff to Orakei Korako thermal area — one of the most interesting and varied in the region. Utilising the abundant thermal energy from within the earth, the Wairakei Thermal Power Station feeds electricity into the national grid. Turn right off SH 1 at the Wairakei Terraces to drive through an area of massive pipes and consider the natural steam rushing through at 200 km/h. Five kilometres south of Wairakei is the turnoff to the spectacular Huka Falls, which is reached after a short easy walk.

Taupo – campground, water activities, walks
Idyllically situated, Taupo is world-renowned as the base for trout fishing on the lake and its tributary rivers. Cafés and bars abound (Bodyfuel on the main street is busy and good), along with opportunities for fine dining, swimming, adventure sports and more sedate activities like a walk through the gardens of the Waipahihi Botanical Reserve. Lake Taupo's waters fill the crater formed by what's believed to be one of the world's largest volcanic eruptions.

13 Rotorua–Taupo SH 5, 27, 1
81 km, 1.5 hours

This route skirts the western edge of Kaingaroa Forest and takes in the major geothermal attractions at Whakarewarewa (3 km from Rotorua), Waimangu (25 km) and Waiotapu (30 km). Golden Springs (43 km) has a motorcamp and thermal baths. Beyond here much of the drive to Wairakei travels between the broad forested avenues formed by the Tahorakuri exotic forest. From Wairakei it's 11 km to Taupo. (See above).

Orakei Korako thermal area

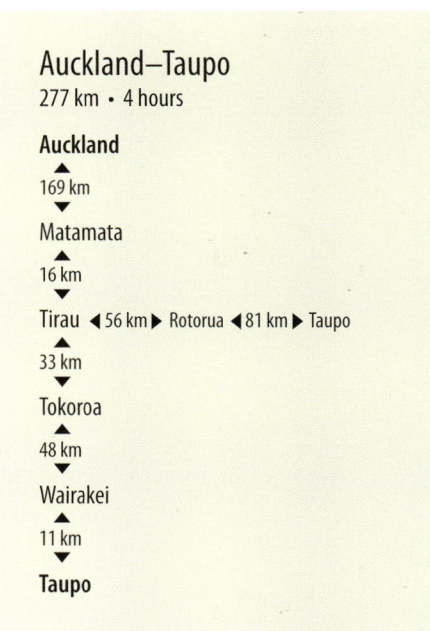

Auckland–Taupo
277 km • 4 hours

Auckland
▲
169 km
▼
Matamata
▲
16 km
▼
Tirau ◄ 56 km ► Rotorua ◄ 81 km ► Taupo
▲
33 km
▼
Tokoroa
▲
48 km
▼
Wairakei
▲
11 km
▼
Taupo

Mt Taranaki

NEW PLYMOUTH

SH3 to Hawera — **Stratford**

SH3 to New Plymouth

Douglas · **Toko**

Waitara River · **Waitara**

43

Onaero

Urenui

3

Pohokura Saddle

Whangamomona Saddle · **Pohokura**

Whangamomona

Mt Messenger

Tongaporutu

Mokau River

Awakino River

Tahora Saddle

Tahora

Tangarakau Gorge

Mokau · Awakino

Parata Saddle

43

3

TAUMARUNUI

Piopio

SH4 to
National Park

4

Eight Mile Junction

SH30 to
Pureora,
Mangakino

Te Kuiti

H A U H U N G A R O A   R A N G E

NORTH

Hamilton–New Plymouth
225 km • 4.5 hours

Hamilton ◄ 94 km ► Kawhai via SH 31

▲
30 km
▼

Te Awamutu

▲
29 km
▼

Otorohanga ◄ 92 km ► Kawhai via Waitomo

▲
20 km
▼

Te Kuiti ◄ 81 km ► Taumarunui

▲   ▲
56 km   156 km
▼   ▼

Awakino   Stratford

▲
59 km
▼

Urenui

▲
31 km
▼

New Plymouth

Marokopa

Marokopa Falls

Te Anga

Mangapohue Arch

Kawhia Harbour

Kawhia

Aotea Harbour

Mt Karioi

itomo Caves

Oparau

Pirongia Mountain

Makomako

Bridal Veil Falls

Te Mata

31

Otorohanga

31

Raglan

Pirongia

39

23

3

Waipa River

Te Awamutu

Whatawhata

Kihikihi

3

HAMILTON

Waikato River

Lake Taupo

SH32 to Turangi

SH41 to Taumarunui

Kuratau Junction

TAUPO

HAUHUNGAROA RANGE

32

PUREORA FOREST

Pureora

Barryville

1

Waikato River

30

Whakamaru

30

Atiamuri

Mangakino

TOKOROA

Lake Arapuni

Putaruru

Maungatautari

Tirau

1

Lake Karapiro

SH27 to Matamata

Karapiro

CAMBRIDGE

Matamata

Hamilton–Taupo
via Pureora Forest
213 km • 3 hours

Hamilton ◀ 55 km ▶ Tirau ◀ 96 km ▶ Taupo

▲
75 km
▼

Te Kuiti

▲
79 km
▼

Mangakino ◀ 98 km ▶ Turangi

▲
28 km
▼

Atiamuri

▲
31 km
▼

Taupo

18 Hamilton–Taupo via Pureora Forest SH 3, 30, 1
213 km, 3 hours

The highlight of this drive is the 78,000-ha Pureora Forest Park, a remnant of the vast podocarp forest that dominated the area before it was logged.

Drive to Te Kuiti via SH 3 (1.25 hours, see Hamilton–New Plymouth, Route 15). From Te Kuiti, turn onto SH 30 which enters the hilly sheep-farming country west of Benneydale village (store, hotel, petrol). East of Benneydale the road passes briefly through the small forested Herekawa Scenic Reserve then reaches Maraeroa Road to Pureora after 20 minutes.

Pureora – campground, walks
Follow the gravel road to the Pureora visitor centre, located, ironically perhaps, in a fragment of native forest inside a plantation forest. The ultimately successful battle to save what was left of the tall trees of Pureora was one of the defining moments in New Zealand's conservation history. Two short walks I would recommend are the Totara Walk and the excellent Forest Tower Walk. Totara Walk (close to the centre) is an easy 30-minute loop amongst the enormous trees the area is known for. A self-guide brochure for tree identification is available. The Forest Tower Walk is signposted from Barryville Road (which returns to SH 30 east of Maraeroa Road). A short walk leads to the 12-metre multilevel forest tower which allows you to climb into the forest canopy and get closer to the raucous native birdlife. Interpretation panels in the tower identify birds and trees.

Mangakino – campground
A settlement with friendly locals on the banks of Lake Maraetai and on the edge of Kinleith Forest. Hot and cold drinks and burgers are sold from a simple bus café on the lakeshore. To reach Taupo, continue along SH 30 beside the Waikato River to the SH 1 junction before Atiamuri.

SH 30 meets SH 32 at Whakamaru (café, fuel). SH 32 links Tokoroa and Turangi between the eastern flanks of the Pureora Forest and the western shores of Lake Taupo. From Whakamaru allow half an hour to reach Tokoroa (north) or 1 hour to the junction with SH 41 at Kuratau (south, the unpretentious Tihoi Trading Post is the only food and drink option along this stretch), and a further half hour to Turangi. From Whakamaru you can continue on SH 30 to SH 1, but a more direct route to Taupo is to drive south on SH 32 for approximately 15 km then take the signposted route on Poihipi Road east to Taupo.

KAIMANAWA MOUNTAINS

Tongariro River

Mt Ngauruhoe

Mt Tongariro

SH1 to
Waiouru

SH47A to
National Park

*Lake
Rotoaira*

SH47 to
National Park

SH1 to
Taupo

TURANGI

Tokaanu

*Lake
Taupo*

Omori

Kuratau

41

Kuratau Junction

SH32 to
Whakamaru

Waituhi
Lookout

41

HAUHUNGAROA

RANGE

21 Ohakune–Wanganui SH 49, 4
110 km, 2 hours

The direct route to Wanganui from Ohakune follows the Mangawhero River on SH 4. However, if you have the time it's worth turning off at Raetihi to take the alternative route via the Whanganui River Road (described below). To get to Raetihi, take SH 49 out of Ohakune for 9 km and turn south onto SH 4 at Tohunga Junction. The stretch of SH 4 from Raetihi is hilly and winding, traversing farmed land above the Mangawhero River much of the way. Thirty kilometres south of Raetihi are the Raukawa Falls, where the 50-metre wide Mangawhero River drops 15 metres over a bluff. They have been described as 'one of the finest waterfalls in New Zealand', and can be seen from a signposted viewing platform off the road. Food and refreshments are available a little further on at Kakatahi, and then at Upokongaro.

Raetihi–Wanganui via the Whanganui River Road
97 km, 2–2.5 hours

An interesting alternative to the SH 4 route is to take the road that follows the Whanganui River (covered by a heritage trail brochure). It is a slow, narrow road, with a 31-km unsealed section from Pipiriki to Koriniti (suitable for campervans, but not caravans). However, it is a very scenic journey, steeped in Maori and European history, with river and forest landscapes, pa, marae and sacred Maori sites. The spiritual and practical relationship Maori had with the river was so important that they named virtually every corner.

Take the road west from Raetihi to reach the Whanganui River at Pipiriki after 30 minutes.

Pipiriki – walks, picnicking, boating
Pipiriki lies on the edge of Whanganui National Park, and is where most kayakers and canoeists from Taumarunui finish their journey. The only food available is take-away style from a caravan (during the busier summer period). There's a 30-minute nature walk from the DoC base (not an information centre), though the easiest way to experience the park is by jetboat – tours can be arranged here.

A jetboat ride to Mangapurua Landing allows you to take the 40-minute walk to the historic 'Bridge to Nowhere'. The bridge over the Mangapurua Stream was opened in 1936 as a link in a proposed road between Raetihi and Taranaki. When the Mangapurua Valley was closed to settlement in 1942, regenerating forest covered the approaches to the bridge, which became known as the 'Bridge to Nowhere'.

Pipiriki–Wanganui
Jerusalem, 11 km from Pipiriki, is most commonly associated with the commune established there by the revered poet James K. Baxter. The beautiful Church of Hiruharama (Jerusalem), built in 1892, features a carved altar of Maori design, kowhaiwhai panels on its walls, and historical information about this remote community.

There is also a convent that was the home of Mother Aubert's mission. The Flying Fox is an isolated, rustic, organic country-stay located across the river and reached by wire-cable.

Beyond Jerusalem, Ranana has a century-old church and a memorial cairn. Nearby Moutoa Island was the site of the Battle of Moutoa in 1864 between Whanganui Maori and invading Hauhau warriors. The site of Operiki Pa, 18 km from Jerusalem, has well-preserved earthworks, and a little further on Koriniti (Corinth) has two restored wharenui (meeting houses) on the marae and a beautiful old church dating from 1865.

There are no shops or service stations though until you reach Upokongaro back on SH 4 where the very new Café Riva offers organic coffee, a brunch menu plus a relaxing garden and live music on occasion. On Thursday–Sunday nights they delight in providing Maori cuisine such as hangi, paua (abalone) and tuna (eel). Perhaps call ahead to make a dinner request.

Whanganui River

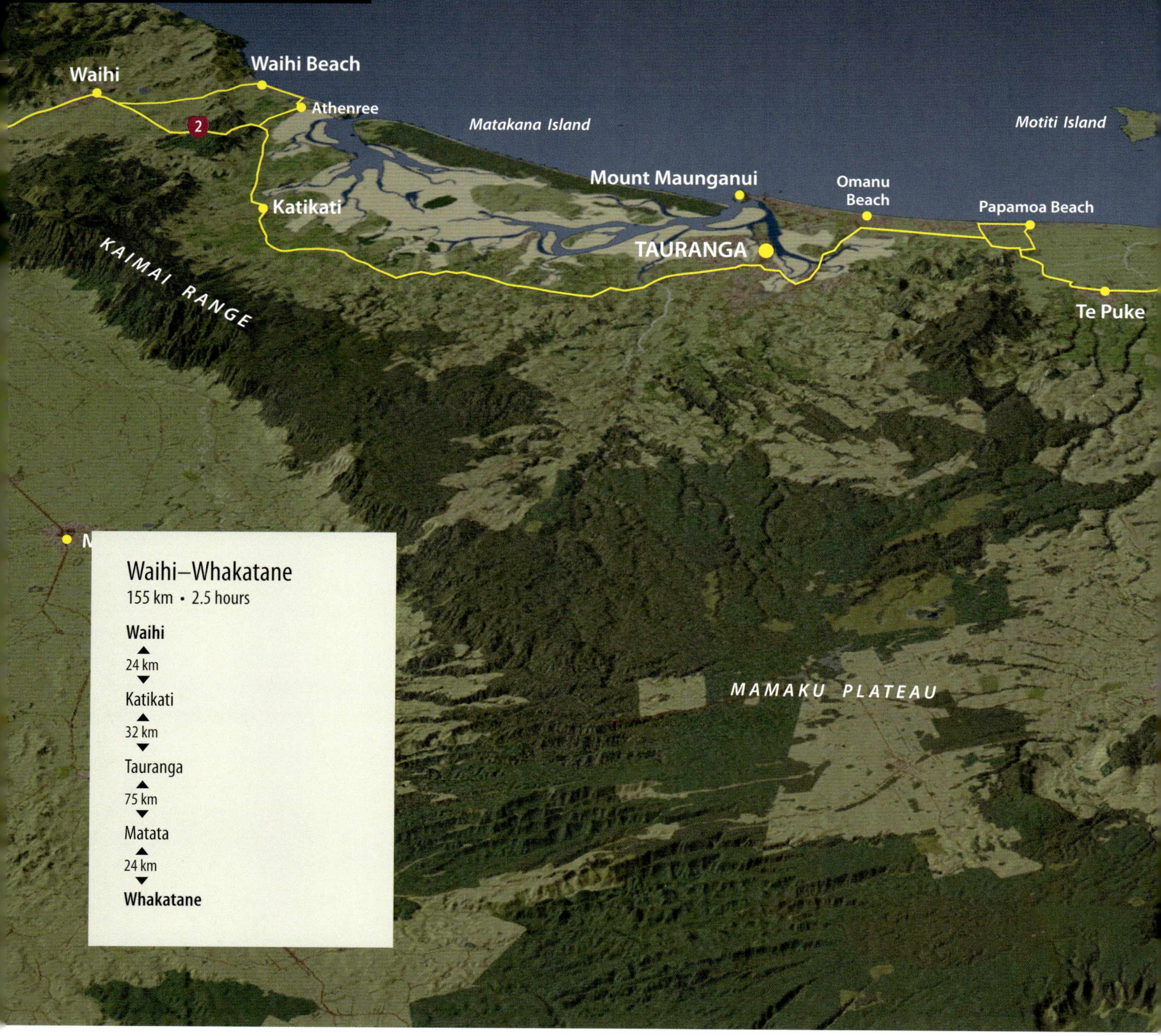

Waihi

Waihi Beach

Athenree

2

Matakana Island

Motiti Island

Katikati

Mount Maunganui

Omanu Beach

Papamoa Beach

KAIMAI RANGE

TAURANGA

Te Puke

Waihi–Whakatane
155 km · 2.5 hours

Waihi
▲
24 km
▼
Katikati
▲
32 km
▼
Tauranga
▲
75 km
▼
Matata
▲
24 km
▼
Whakatane

MAMAKU PLATEAU

22 Waihi–Whakatane SH 2
155 km, 2.5 hours

A drive through the hills and coastal plains of Bay of Plenty, passing Tauranga and resorts at Waihi Beach, Mount Maunganui and Ohope along the way. SH 2 is a busy road which services the region's market gardening, fruitgrowing and forestry industries.

Waihi Beach – campground, swimming
The turnoff to Waihi Beach is 4 km from Waihi. Waihi Beach occupies a lengthy sweep of coast south of Waihi. Between Waihi Beach settlement and the Bowentown Heads are safe swimming beaches, good surfing, hot pools at Athenree, camping, and a walk to Orokawa Bay at the north end of the beach. The Flat

White café/restaurant located on the beachfront on Shaw Road is the best bet for a good meal, followed closely by the Hot Pipi Café. On Emerton Road near Athenree you will find the shabby exterior of the Swell Café but the interior is okay and the coffee is even better.

Back on SH 2 the road skirts Tauranga Harbour through to Katikati, Tauranga and Mount Maunganui. Look for the Twickenham Café and gardens on the northern outskirts of Katikati which makes yummy cakes (especially the sticky date pudding!) and excellent coffee. Katikati is known for the many wall-sized murals depicting the history of the area. Wineries worth noting are Katikati's Morton Estate and Bethlehem's Mills Reef winery and restaurant (just before entering Tauranga).

Bay of Plenty

Moutohora Island

aketu

Matata

WHAKATANE

2

Edgecumbe

33

NORTH

2

Te Teko

Lake
Rotoehu

Lake
Rotoma

30

SH33

Lake Rotoma

KAWERAU

Lake Rotoiti

30

Ruato

Tikitere

Te Ngae

Lake
Okataina

Lake
Rotorua

Lake
Okareka

*Lake
Tarawera*

ROTORUA

Te Wairoa

Lake
Tikitapu

Lake
Rotokakahi

Rotorua–Whakatane
86 km · 1.5 hours

Rotorua

▲
16 km
▼

Te Ngae

▲
25 km
▼

Lake Rotoma

▲
45 km
▼

Whakatane

Mount Maunganui

Mount Maunganui – campground, walks, swimming

Mount Maunganui (turn off SH 2 at Omanu Beach) has become a rather glitzy resort with any number of beachfront cafés. The beach is splendid while walks on the Mount offer outstanding coastal views over Tauranga Harbour, Matakana Island and the Bay of Plenty. Climbing the Mount will take around 1 hour 20 minutes while the nearby Mt Drury is an easier 20 minutes and good for a picnic.

Papamoa Beach/Te Puke – campground, swimming

Papamoa Beach has a rapidly developing resort village and retirement haven, complete with shopping mall. On the beachfront is a nicely situated campground and the Blue Bijou café. Te Puke's Deli Café in the town centre is the pick of eating options here.

Te Puke to Whakatane takes 30 minutes (turn off SH 2 at Matamata).

Whakatane

Whakatane's main drawcard lies offshore in the Bay of Plenty – White Island. This small island is New Zealand's only continuously active volcano and can be explored during boat or helicopter tours. White Island is also one of the world's best scuba diving destinations, with large schools of fish attracted by the underwater steam vents. Peejay's is the longest established boat operator and also has a café. The Bean, in Strand East, is the recommended café in town.

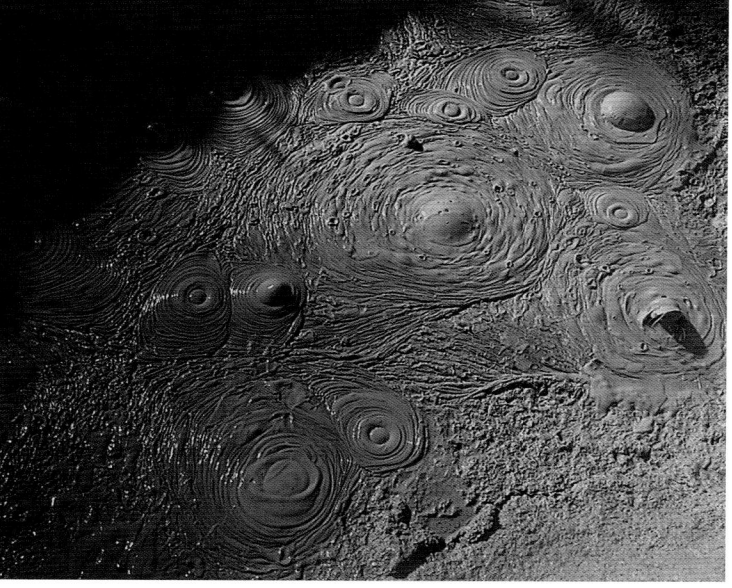

Mudpool at Tikitere

23 Rotorua–Whakatane SH 30
86 km, 1.5 hours (see map previous page)

The string of beautiful lakes between Rotorua and Whakatane is the highlight of this drive. You could spend any amount of time swimming, picnicking, fishing, boating or walking at these lakes, which also have high natural and cultural values.

Rotorua

Rotorua has long been a tourist destination, and people have been coming to 'take the waters' in the city's spas since the nineteenth century. The historic Bath House is now the Rotorua Museum of Art and History, and has a viewing platform on the roof with panoramic views over the adjacent Government Gardens, the city and Lake Rotorua.

It's hard to escape the distinctive smell of sulphur in Rotorua, an unmistakable sign that you are in the middle of an active volcanic area. The geothermal areas in the region include geysers, hot pools, volcanic lakes, coloured mineral terraces and boiling mud. Waiotapu Thermal Wonderland, 25 km south of Rotorua on SH 5, is one of the best of these places to visit.

Rotorua is also a major centre for Maori culture, and home of the Maori Arts and Crafts Institute where woodcarvers, weavers and greenstone sculptors are trained in traditional techniques. The local Te Arawa tribe has run tourist enterprises for more than a century, and there are opportunities to take in Maori cultural performances and sample traditional food; as well as demonstrations by expert carvers and weavers.

One way to combine Rotorua's attractions is to visit the Whakarewarewa Thermal Village at the southern end of the city. Here, surrounded by erupting geysers, bubbling mud pools and hot thermal springs, you can experience a traditional Maori village lifestyle and taste food cooked in a hangi (earth oven).

Lakes Okareka, Tikitapu, Rotokakahi & Tarawera – campground, walks, water recreation

This sequence of lakes is reached by turning off SH 30 at Lynmore, 3 km from Rotorua by Whakarewarewa Forest Park. The lakes are well signposted and are reached along sealed roads. Lakes Tikitapu and Okareka are both 11 km from Rotorua. Tikitapu has a campground and store and at its southern end is a viewpoint which also overlooks Rotokakahi. Lake Okareka offers picnicking in a quiet reserve. The Te Wairoa buried village is reached shortly before Lake Tarawera after a pleasant forested drive. Here there is a café, museum and tours of the village. At Lake Tarawera Landing, opposite the café, is a short 3-minute walk to some early Maori rock drawings (not signposted).

Back on SH 30, the route skirts the eastern shores of Lake Rotorua then turns inland towards Lake Rotoiti. (SH 33 to Te Puke turns off at Te Ngae – allow 40 minutes.)

Tikitere (Hells Gate Thermal Reserve) – walks, picnicking

Not far from Te Ngae is this iwi-owned thermal reserve, the most active thermal area in the region. Rotorua's only mud volcano and the largest hot waterfall in this hemisphere are among its attractions, as well as the Wai Ora spa with mineral-rich mud to wallow in.

Lakes Rotoiti, Rotoehu, Okataina & Rotoma – walks, picnicking, water recreation

A picnic area at the eastern end of Lake Rotoiti also has an easy track to the more secluded Lake Rotoehu. Halfway around Lake Rotoiti at Ruato is the turnoff to Lake Okataina, perhaps the prettiest of the lakes with its native forest surrounds. There are a number of short forest walks from the road end. There is a campground at Lake Rotoma.

From Rotoma, SH 30 descends through native forests and pine plantations, past the loop road to Kawerau, and onto the Rangitaiki River plains to Whakatane.

24 Whakatane–Opotiki via Wainui Road
42 km, 1 hour (see map overleaf)

SH 2 bypasses Whakatane on the way to Opotiki, so the quicker and more scenic route between the two is to take the Wainui Road around Ohiwa Harbour. Ohope, 8 km from Whakatane, is a popular holiday spot with 11 km of beach – try the Café Surfside.

Just past Ohope is the easy 1-hour walk around the Tauwhare Pa, once a fortified village, which overlooks Ohiwa Harbour. The pa has a fascinating history and offers fine views and birdwatching.

Opotiki – campground, walks, swimming

Arching groves of pohutukawa enfold the highway as it nears Opotiki. A few minutes from the town on a roadside reserve are the arresting carved pou whenua Te Ara Ki Te Tairawhiti, the 'Pathway to the Sunrise' by artist Heke Collier, whose work is also found on Opotiki's main street. Those who require sustenance should try the excellent Two Fish café on Church Street (main shopping street).

Pohutu geyser, Rotorua

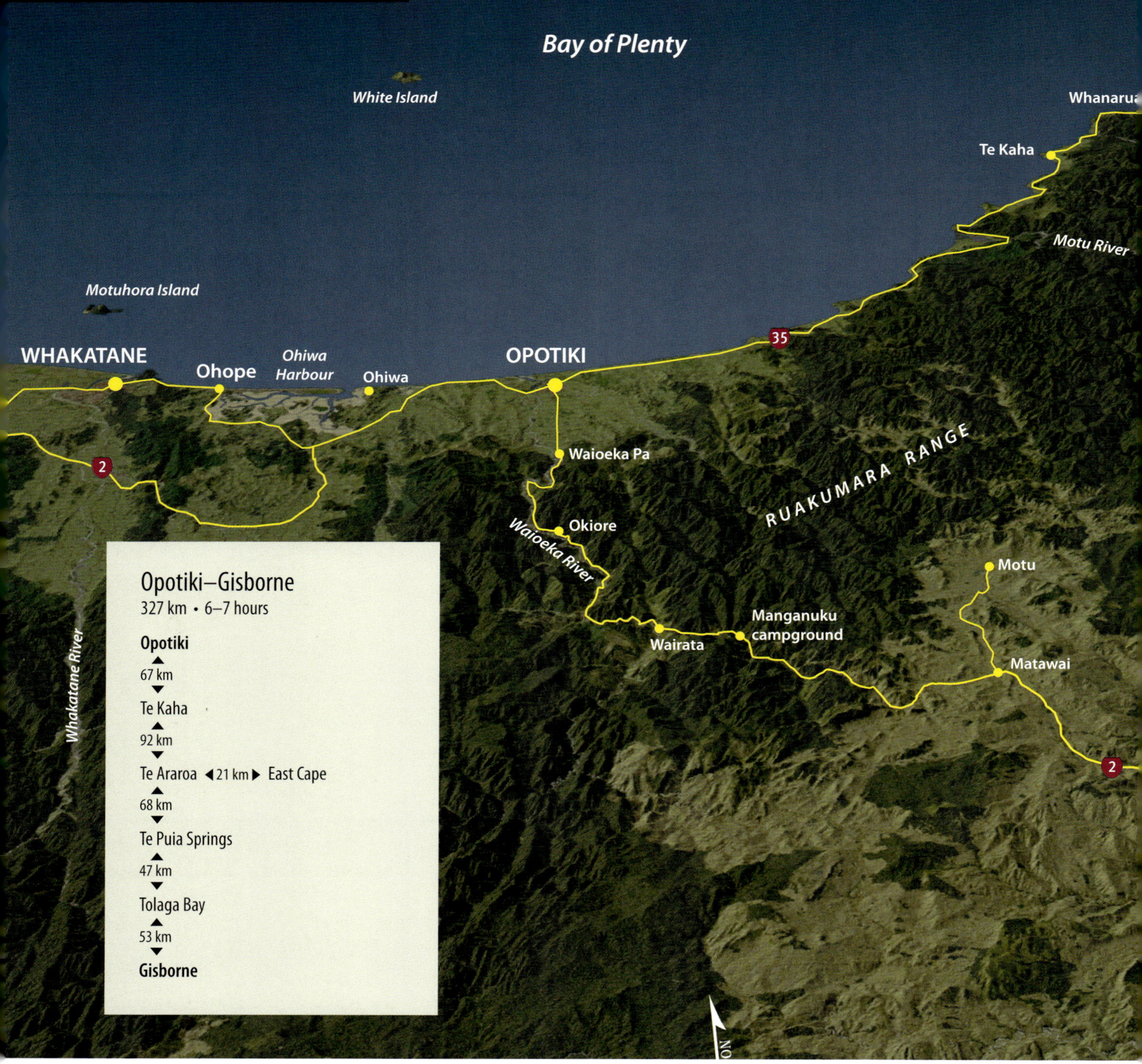

Bay of Plenty

White Island

Whanarua

Te Kaha

Motu River

Motuhora Island

WHAKATANE

Ohope

Ohiwa Harbour

Ohiwa

OPOTIKI

35

Waioeka Pa

2

Waioeka River

Okiore

RUAKUMARA RANGE

Motu

Manganuku campground

Wairata

Matawai

Whakatane River

2

Opotiki–Gisborne
327 km • 6–7 hours

Opotiki
▲
67 km
▼
Te Kaha
▲
92 km
▼
Te Araroa ◄21 km► East Cape
▲
68 km
▼
Te Puia Springs
▲
47 km
▼
Tolaga Bay
▲
53 km
▼
Gisborne

25 Opotiki–Gisborne SH 35

327 km, 6–7 hours

The drive around East Cape from Opotiki to Gisborne is one of the most memorable in New Zealand. Here, Maori communities have steadfastly maintained links with their culture, history and landscape. Evidence of this is everywhere in the numerous marae with their distinctive carved or painted wharenui (meeting houses), and in their memorials and schools. You can't just walk onto a marae – here and anywhere else in the country prior permission must be granted and appropriate welcomes offered to visitors – not something organised lightly. But you never know, a chat with a friendly local can do wonders.

European history, particularly that associated with Captain James Cook, is another distinctive feature of the region. This history is recounted in numerous places: the Cook Landing Site National Historic Reserve in Gisborne, the wharf at Tolaga Bay, and the beautiful Tikitiki Church in which the melding of European and Maori culture is evocatively illustrated.

Most settlements have a store, but for the passing traveller petrol is expensive and tearoom food is produced from pie warmers and vats of fat. The key to truly rewarding experiences on the Cape is to spend a night or two with locals like Paul and Maryanne of Te Kaha Lodge, which is likely to yield splendid kaimoana (seafood) and hospitality – kia ora!

Between Labour Weekend (last weekend in October) and Easter it is

Opotiki–Gisborne
via the Waioeka Gorge
142 km • 2.5 hours

Opotiki
▲
70 km
▼
Matawai ◄18 km► Motu
▲
41 km
▼
Te Karaka
▲
31 km
▼
Gisborne

Cape Runaway

Hicks Bay

Te Araroa

35

Tokata

East Cape

Oruaiti Beach

Waihau Bay

Tikitiki

Waiapu River

Ruatoria

Mt Hikurangi

Waipiro Bay

Te Puia Springs

Waima

Tokomaru Bay

Anaura Bay

Karaka Bay

35

Cooks Cove

Tolaga Bay

Te Karaka

Waihuka River

Ormond

Pouawa

GISBORNE

possible to freedom camp at Waipiro Bay, Tokomaru Bay, Kaiaua Beach, Tolaga Bay, Waihau Bay, Pouawa and Turihawa Beach. Watch out for stock (especially cattle) wandering on the roads.

Opotiki–Whangaparaoa, 118 km
This first leg of SH 35 more or less hugs the Bay of Plenty coast as far as Whangaparaoa, in places cutting high onto bluffs and hills, allowing views of the spectacular land and seascape, and into the forested Raukumara hinterland. Beaches and campgrounds reinforce the holiday feel of this coastal section of the highway where there are numerous places to camp, swim, fish, snorkel, dive, picnic or go horse trekking.

Opape/Marenui Hill/Omaio – beaches, walks, camping
Opape is worth noting for the new Tauturangi Walkway (signposted, brochure available, 40 minutes to an hour return, great coastal views). Maraenui Hill 20 km from Opape offers a spectacular outlook before the road descends to cross the wide and beautiful Motu River. Free camping is allowed at the Omaio Reserve.

Te Kaha – campground, swimming, fishing
Once a whaling village, Te Kaha is these days a popular holiday destination with safe swimming and fishing, a store (serving

espresso coffee), splendid meeting house and what remains of a redoubt at Te Kaha Tukaki marae.

Whanarua Bay – campground, picnicking, swimming, fishing

Claimed to have its own microclimate, the bay's central attractions are its secluded beaches, swimming and fishing, and coastal views from Karirangi Hill including White Island. The Pacific Macadamia Nut Farm sells a range of macadamia products, and also runs a small café offering a healthier line of food including panini and scrummy muffins.

Raukokore

Located by the ocean at Raukokore is a very attractive church built in 1894. Take a look inside to understand something of the local Christian Maori community.

Waihau Bay – campground, picnicking, swimming, fishing

Another popular destination with a store/tearooms where you can get a good breakfast fry-up. At Orete Point near the Waihau Bay Lodge (really just a flash pub) is a plaque commemorating the fact that in 1897 'nothing happened'. Nearby Oruaiti Beach is considered the best on this stretch.

Whangaparaoa

Steeped in Maori history, Whangaparaoa has a reinstated pa and meeting house open to visitors, while guided historic tours of the area over Maori land are also offered. The beach at Whangaparaoa Bay is said to be where the Tainui and Arawa canoes landed with their cargo of colonisers from Hawaiiki circa 1350 AD.

Whangaparaoa–Gisborne, 209 km

South of Cape Runaway is the Ngati Porou tribal area. From Whangaparaoa, SH 35 remains inland for much of the route to Gisborne, the exceptions being sections from Hicks Bay to Te Araroa and Pouawa to Gisborne.

Hicks Bay

Hicks Bay occupies an important place in the history of Ngati Porou, whose people have lived here for up to 1000 years. There are many historic sites and excavated fortifications. Tuwhakairi-ora meeting house, 'one of the finest in the East Cape', was named after a famous warrior to whom the area's original families trace their lineage. St Barnabas Church (1979) in the marae grounds is embellished with Maori art and exhibits a marriage of traditional and recent architecture.

Te Araroa

From Hicks Bay the road presents excellent views over the coast before the descent to the Tokata Flats where there is a holiday park. Soon after is the coastal settlement of Te Araroa (store, fuel). What is claimed to be the country's oldest (at least 350 years) and largest pohutukawa (named Te Waha-o-Rerekohu)

stands on the edge of Hinerupe Marae on the beachfront. Take-aways are the only option here.

East Cape Lighthouse – walk

From Te Araroa you can drive to the New Zealand mainland's most easterly point and climb the several hundred steps to the East Cape Lighthouse atop Otiki Hill (40 km return, half unsealed, 20 minutes one way. Watch out for wandering stock and horses). The track crosses Ngati Porou land and, although permission isn't required, a small koha (donation) is requested.

Tikitiki

Between Te Araroa and Tikitiki, SH 35 traverses rural and forest landscapes and climbs high onto a ridge offering views of the Raukumara Range and the Waiapu Mountains – the sacred peaks of Ngati Porou – the highest and most important of these being Mt Hikurangi (1752 m). On a fine day Hikurangi can be seen from many places between Tikitiki and Te Puia.

Tikitiki on the north bank of the Waiapu River is where the beautiful St Mary's Church is located, with an interior of carved panels and flax weavings. Like Hicks Bay, excavated fortifications dating to the 1860 land wars are found on the hill above the settlement.

Ruatoria

Nineteen kilometres further is Ruatoria, one of East Cape's largest settlements, dominated by views of Mt Hikurangi and nearby peaks. Try Sunburst Café for lunch and coffee. People of Ngati Porou tribe operate a number of businesses in this town including a small visitor centre where you will find exquisitely carved creations by a Ngati Porou artist. Tours by 4WD up Mt Hikurangi guided by local people are an excellent introduction to the history and legend of Ngati Porou.

South of Ruatoria, enquire at the Te Puia Springs Hotel about a private dip in their natural, mineral-rich hot pool ($5 for 30 minutes, bring a towel).

Tokomaru Bay – swimming

The welcoming sweep of Tokomaru Bay is reached 11 km from Te Puia. As well as catering for holidaymakers with accommodation and a store, Tokomaru Bay is a favoured haunt of fishers and local artists and crafts people. There is a safe beach, and the Te Puka Tavern on the road east towards Waima is just a few metres from the sea. There are four marae at the bay including Pakirikiri Marae (1934) which has a large carved meeting house.

Anaura Bay – campground, walks

From Tokomaru Bay the road returns inland and climbs high through prime East Cape sheep farming country. Anaura Bay, a 7-km diversion from SH 35 about 22 km from Tokomaru Bay, has a campground and a 3.5 km coastal walkway through farmland and forest.

Tolaga Bay – walks

Tolaga Bay (36 km from Tokomaru Bay, 53 km from Gisborne) is renowned for the 700-metre concrete jetty at the bay's southern end. Completed in 1929, the jetty serviced coastal shipping until 1967. Though in need of restoration the jetty is still used by recreational fishers or those who want a stroll. Near the wharf is the Cooks Cove walkway (allow 2–3 hours) through farm and forest and along cliff tops to a lookout, the Hole in the Wall and Cooks Cove itself. A memorial records the visit of Captain Cook to Tolaga Bay in October 1769.

Pouawa–Gisborne

At Pouawa is the Te Tapuwae o Rongokako marine reserve which is administered by the Department of Conservation, local iwi, and recreational and commercial fishers. Pouawa is a popular free-camping, swimming and diving area, though fishing is banned in the reserve. The drive to Gisborne follows the Pacific coast through several small settlements and past formal and informal camping sites on the edge of surf and swimming beaches.

Gisborne

As the most easterly city in the world Gisborne is the first to wake up to a new day. Captain Cook was the first European to set foot on these islands, back in 1769, and he did so on the Gisborne waterfront. A memorial marks the spot on Kaiti Beach. My pick of the cafés is the Fruit Bistro on Peel Street – tiny but good. Otherwise try the 1874 Café in the Poverty Bay Club building at the eastern end of Childers Road. Umaini Deli on Grey Street comes in third. The Tairawhiti Museum has an interesting display about the Maori Battalion's exploits and sacrifices during WWII. Surfers should head for Centennial Marine Drive and some very popular waves. The information centre is on Grey Street.

26 Opotiki–Gisborne via the Waioeka Gorge SH 2
142 km, 2.5 hours (see map previous page)

The highlight of this route is the 45-km Waioeka Gorge which begins 14 km south of Opotiki.

Waioeka Gorge

At the entrance to the gorge is Waioeka River Kayak company offering easy 2-hour trips on the river. Into the gorge and following the Waioeka River, the road winds between the steep forested flanks of the Huiarau and Raukumara ranges. Three kilometres from the kayak operation is the Waioeka nature trail, a worthwhile and easy 15-minute interpreted forest walk.

Seven kilometres further is the start of the Tauranga Track where an easy 6-minute walk leads to a recently restored historic suspension bridge. The Manganuku campground (DoC), 47 km from Opotiki, has toilets and barbecue sites, and is the start of a couple of longer tramping routes.

Matawai – campground

After the campground the highway leaves the gorge and ascends Traffords Hill then crosses into the upper reaches of the Motu River to Matawai village. The 14-km diversion north from Matawai to Motu is of interest for those keen on horsetrekking, mountain-biking, walking, rafting and fishing. After another 4 km (unsealed) you will find the 2-hour (each way) Whinray Reserve Bush Walk, which starts by crossing a large swingbridge overlooking the impressive Motu Falls.

Te Karaka

Back on SH 2 the journey to Gisborne follows the Waihuka River, passing Otoko (where you can take a walk along the Otoko Walkway – all that remains of the old Moutohora railway link to Gisborne) and Te Karaka on the Poverty Bay river flats.

Ormond

Towards Ormond you enter Gisborne's prosperous horticultural and wine-growing area. Along this stretch is the so-called 'slope of gold' chardonnay-growing area. A number of wineries are located hereabouts including Longbush, TW, Acton Estate and the Pouparae Park boutique winery. Wine tastings at these wineries are by appointment only. Montana's wines can be tasted at their shop on Lyttons Road in Gisborne. (For locations of other wineries, get a winery map from the Gisborne information centre and ask about drive-by tasting opportunities.)

Memorial Hall, Ruatoria

ROTORUA

SH5 to Taupo

38

KAINGAROA FOREST

Murupara

IKAWHENUA RANGE

Rangitaiki River

Whakatane River

Te Whaiti

Ruatahuna

Minginui

HUIARAU RANGE

Aniwaniwa

NORTH

Lake Waikaremoana

Onepoto

Tuai

Waiau River

Mohaka River

Rotorua–Wairoa

222 km • 5 hours

Rotorua
▲
63 km
▼
Murupara
▲
49 km
▼
Ruatahuna
▲
45 km
▼
Aniwaniwa
▲
65 km
▼
Wairoa

WHAKATANE

HUIARAU RANGE

ake Waikareiti

38

Frasertown

Wairoa River

WAIROA

27 Rotorua–Waikaremoana–Wairoa
SH 5, 38 and 86 km of unsealed road
222 km, 5 hours

On the plus side, the road to Lake Waikaremoana ranks as one of the most scenic in this book, involving, by my estimation, the longest forest drive in New Zealand – the 102 km between Murupara and Onepoto at Lake Waikaremoana in Te Urewera National Park. The area is remote, covered in dense podocarp and beech forest, and resounds with Maori history and culture. On the negative, the route is mostly unsealed and often narrow, locals drive it too fast, and unfortunately some tourists can't handle the hazards. That said, by New Zealand standards of unsealed roads, it rates as one of the better ones for road surface. Campervans can make the journey, but check your insurance first (as should drivers of all rentals).

From Rotorua take SH 5 to the SH 38 junction (26 km) and proceed through Kaingaroa Forest to Murupara (1 hour).

Murupara
Visit the DoC office here for information on the road, camping sites, and walks. Allow 2 hours to reach Aniwaniwa (excluding sightseeing!) from Murupara. Beyond Murupara the road approaches the barrier of hills formed by the Te Urewera ranges, passing a sign indicating a winding road for a mere 120 km. The tarmac ends not far past the turnoff to Minginui and Whirinaki Forest Park (an outstanding podocarp reserve with a roadend campground and many rewarding forest walks).

Ruatahuna
A farming locality cleared from the forest, and traditional centre of the Tuhoe people who have inhabited the Te Urewera ranges for hundreds of years. Whole families on horseback driving stock is a diverting and not uncommon sight around these parts. From Ruatahuna the road climbs to Papiiora Ridge with fine views of ranges and forest. You'll spot the Mokau Stream waterfall across the valley then, as you drive around and across the stream, look back across the valley at the smaller waterfall opposite. The road then crosses Taupeupe Saddle (919 m) on the crest of the Huiarau Range from where the rivers and the road drop toward the northern arm of Lake Waikaremoana.

Aniwaniwa Visitor Centre – campground, walks
The descent to and drive around the lake to Aniwaniwa is one of increasingly beautiful vistas. There are several roadside camping sites on this section. At Aniwaniwa, the national park information centre provides an absorbing interpretation of the natural and cultural values of this region. From the visitor centre the road continues along the eastern shore until the forest abruptly ends and the road descends steeply to Tuai. At Tuai is the incongruous Rangers Café and Bar (saddles on bar stools, yee-ha) with adjacent accommodation and campsites.

Allow 1 hour to Wairoa from Tuai. The café options in Wairoa are not impressive: first try the Greenhouse Garden Centre (which also has a café) on Mahia Avenue (the road that enters Wairoa, just past the right turn to the town centre). Otherwise, Oslers Bakery on Marine Parade won the Best NZ Baker competition in 2005 and 2006.

53

HUIARAUA RANGE

Lake Waikaremoana

SH38 to Waikaremoana

Mohaka River

2

Boundary Stream scenic reserve

Putorino

Tutira

Lake Tutira

Esk River

TANGOIO FOREST

Tangoio

2

SH5 to Napier

NAPIER

Tutaekuri River

Ngaruroro River

Wairoa–Napier
119 km • 2 hours

Wairoa
▲
75 km
▼
Tutira
▲
21 km
▼
Tangoio
▲
23 km
▼
Napier

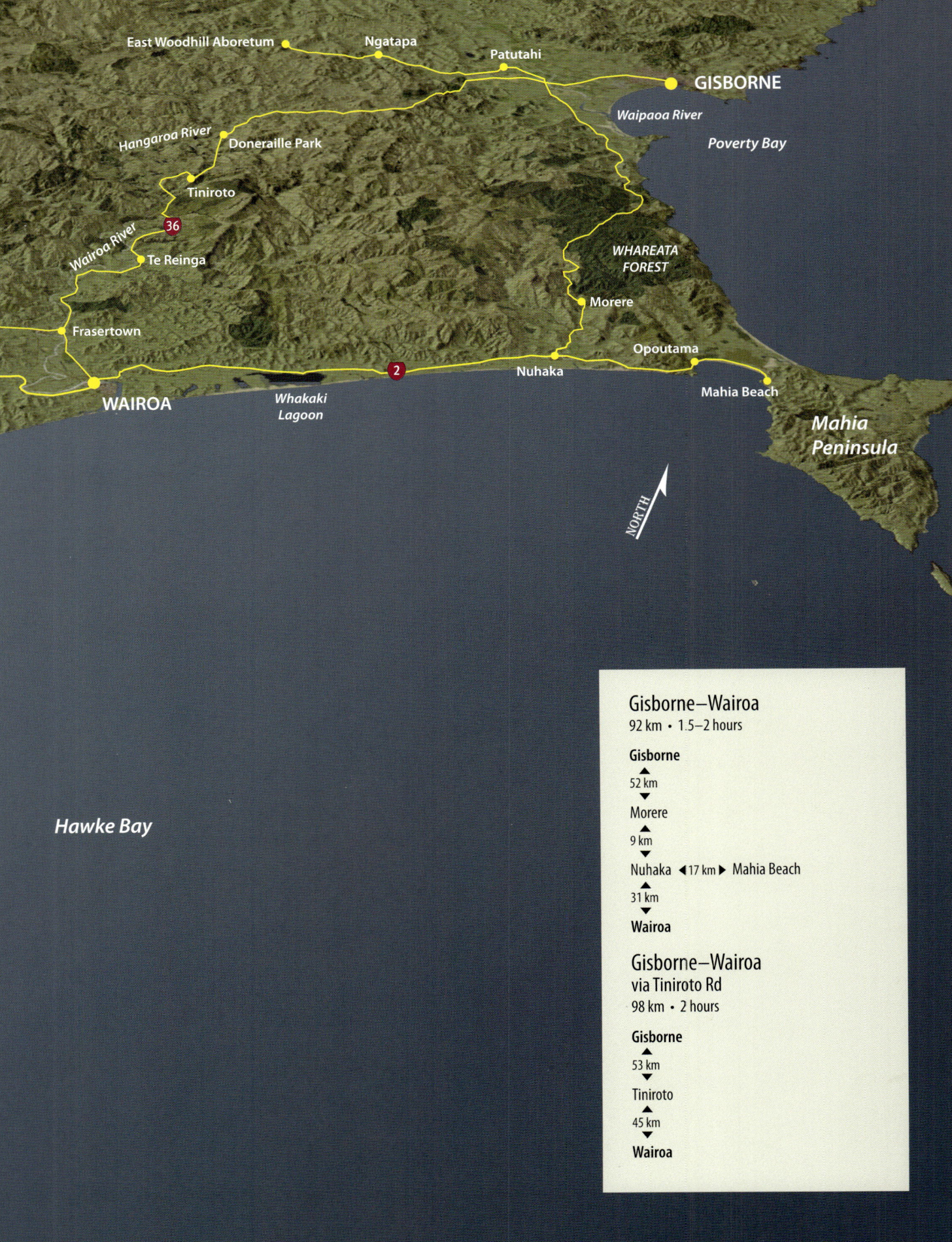

East Woodhill Aboretum
Ngatapa
Patutahi
GISBORNE
Waipaoa River
Poverty Bay
Hangaroa River
Doneraille Park
Tiniroto
Wairoa River
36
Te Reinga
WHAREATA FOREST
Morere
Frasertown
2
Opoutama
Nuhaka
Mahia Beach
WAIROA
Whakaki Lagoon
Mahia Peninsula
Hawke Bay

NORTH

Gisborne–Wairoa
92 km • 1.5–2 hours

Gisborne
▲
52 km
▼
Morere
▲
9 km
▼
Nuhaka ◀17 km▶ Mahia Beach
▲
31 km
▼
Wairoa

Gisborne–Wairoa
via Tiniroto Rd
98 km • 2 hours

Gisborne
▲
53 km
▼
Tiniroto
▲
45 km
▼
Wairoa

28 Gisborne–Wairoa SH 2
92 km, 1.5–2 hours (see map previous page)

Before departing from Gisborne, a worthwhile diversion is to visit the internationally renowned Eastwoodhill Arboretum (35 km from Gisborne, sealed road) by driving west through Matawhero then turning right where signposted to Ngatapa. More than 15,000 trees from New Zealand, North America and Europe create a natural playground with picnic areas and walking tracks. Roughly 12 km beyond Eastwoodhill you will find the Rere Falls (picnics) and natural rockslide – good fun for the adventurous.

From Gisborne SH 2 enters the Poverty Bay flats through the Matawhero wine-growing area, and heads south towards the large Wharerata pine plantation and Mahia Peninsula.

 Morere – hot springs, campground, walks

Morere hot springs, 52 km from Gisborne at the south end of Wharerata forest, is an attractively laid out spa in a 200-ha native forest reserve. As well as a variety of public and private thermal pools, the reserve has a number of forest walks. A great place for a pause, or an overnight stop as accommodation is also available.

 Mahia Peninsula – campgrounds, walks, surfing, swimming

At Nuhaka is the turnoff to the Mahia Peninsula, a very popular surfing, swimming and holiday destination. Mahia Beach settlement is 17 km from Nuhaka at the south end of Opoutama Beach. The drive there is sealed and offers fine views along the peninsula, and is particularly dramatic in the evenings when a strong swell is running and low sun lights the clifflines. Beyond Mahia Beach the sealed road, now somewhat narrower, continues to Oraka Beach and Mahia on the peninsula's eastern side. Check the interesting sedimentary formations in the intertidal zone, also a popular area for surfers.

Back on SH 2 it's a straight run west past Whakaki Lagoon into Wairoa.

29 Gisborne–Wairoa via Tiniroto SH 36 (The Tiniroto Road)
98 km, 1.5–2 hours (see map previous page)

This alternative route to SH 2 winds through the hilly and often spectacular rural hinterland west of Gisborne. The road is sealed and narrow in places. Highlights include Doneraille Park (47 km from Gisborne), a forest reserve next to the Hangaroa River, with safe swimming, a campground and toilets. Three unsealed kilometres inland from Tiniroto is Hackfalls Arboretum which has a collection of more than 3000 tree species, including oaks, poplars and maples, spread over 100 acres.

Te Reinga Falls is in one of the few scraps of native forest left in the area, a short distance along Ruakituri Valley Road from Te Reinga. The impressive 18-metre falls tumble over a sandstone bluff into a narrow gorge which can be viewed from a well-located platform. Frasertown (91 km from Gisborne, 7 km from Wairoa) is a small town at the junction with SH 38 which leads to Te Urewera National Park. (See Rotorua–Wairoa, Route 27.)

Pohutukawa flowering at Wainui Beach, Gisborne

30 Wairoa–Napier SH 2
119 km, 2 hours (see map previous page)

This route traverses the hilly rural hinterland between Wairoa and Napier, passing several small settlements and high points with views toward Hawke Bay. Closer to Napier are several interesting reserves: Lake Tutira, White Pine Bush and Tangoio. Just south of Wairoa you will find Café 287, with good coffee and cake. After the small settlement of Raupunga you pass beneath a steel railbridge built in 1937 and 95 metres high. Continuing on, you may spot the sign (south of Putorino) pointing to Shine Falls. To reach the 58-metre falls follow the track across farmland (leave gates as you find them) beneath towering sandstone cliffs and through native bush (2 hours return).

 Lake Tutira – picnicking, swimming, walks, fishing
Seventy-five kilometres from Wairoa, the Lake Tutira wildlife refuge and its environs occupies a special place in New Zealand conservation history thanks to the efforts of a pioneer farmer and conservationist Herbert Guthrie Smith. A carpark at the southern end provides access to a pleasant picnic site and the start of several walking tracks.

 Boundary Stream Scenic Reserve – walks
Boundary Stream, a 700-ha forest remnant north of Tutira (75 km from Wairoa) is one of six 'mainland islands' established by the Department of Conservation. The 'mainland island' concept involves a determined effort to reduce introduced pests such as rats, stoats and possums to enable native plants and animals to recover, and even allow the re-introduction of endangered species that might otherwise only survive on islands offshore. Although such islands involve a long-range view, in just a few years there are encouraging signs that birdlife and forest species are staging a recovery at Boundary Stream. To reach the reserve, turn onto Matahorua Road by the Tutira store. For an interesting walk, take the lefthand fork (about 6 km from the store) onto Pohukura Road and drive to the Kamahi Loop track, a 2-hour loop through a varied lowland podocarp and kamahi forest.

 White Pine Bush/ Tangoio Falls – picnicking, walks
A 19-ha forest remnant 96 km from Wairoa features tall kahikatea (white pine) and other rainforest trees that once covered the rest of the surrounding landscape. A 30-minute loop through the forest (best done anticlockwise) is accessible to wheelchairs. Two kilometres on is the Tangoio Falls Scenic Reserve where there is a 20-minute forest walk to Te Ana Falls. A streamside track links White Pine Bush and the Tangoio Falls carpark (1.5 hours one way).

From here SH 2 winds through pine forest to reach the Hawke Bay coastline just past Tangoio settlement, 23 km from Napier. As you approach Napier the Pacific Ocean provides a great view to the east, while to the west some very low-lying farmland and wetland attracts a variety of birdlife. There is little opportunity to stop and enjoy this natural area until you pass the airport, where a signposted track explores the fringes of a section of bird-friendly reserve. Napier, being a larger centre, has any number of cafés and restaurants to choose from. In the city my choice is Café Devine, but the essence of this region lies in the sumptuous collection of wineries surrounding Napier and Hastings, many with their own excellent cafés or restaurants.

Kahikatea trees, White Pine Bush

Oakura

45

Puniho

Warea

Okato

Pungarehu

45

North Egmont

Mt Taranaki

East Egmont

Dawson Falls

Kaponga

Eltham

Waingongoro River

3

to
Manaia,
Ounake,
Oaonui

45

Normanby

HAWERA

SH3 to
Wanganui

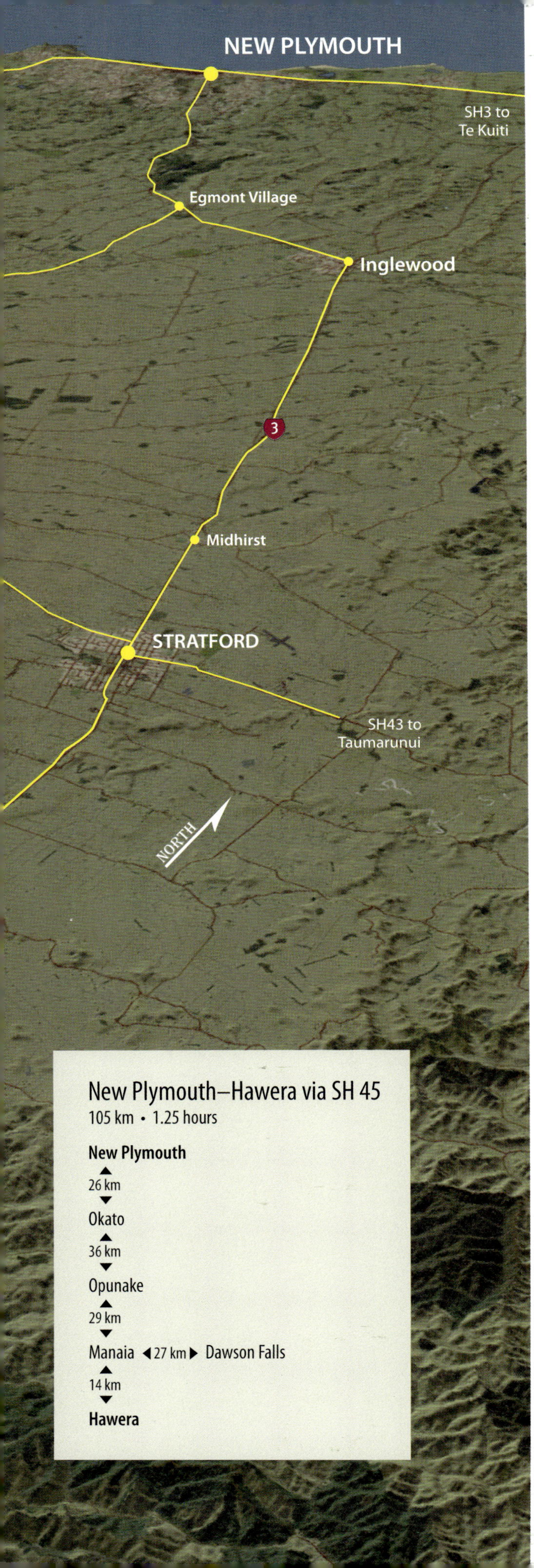

SH3 to
Te Kuiti

Egmont Village

Inglewood

3

Midhirst

STRATFORD

SH43 to
Taumarunui

NORTH

New Plymouth–Hawera via SH 45

105 km • 1.25 hours

New Plymouth
▲
▼
26 km

Okato
▲
▼
36 km

Opunake
▲
▼
29 km

Manaia ◄27 km► Dawson Falls
▲
▼
14 km

Hawera

31 New Plymouth–Hawera via SH 45

105 km, 1.25 hours

The 'Surf Highway' is a great scenic drive around the western side of Mt Taranaki. Highlights are surfing and swimming beaches, Pukeiti Gardens, views of Mt Taranaki and Opunake's Sugar Juice Café.

Oakura – campground
Oakura, 15 km from New Plymouth, is Taranaki's most popular beach resort, with a family friendly beach, excellent swimming and surfing, picnic sites and patrolled swimming areas. The Green Ginger Café is the pick of the cafés here.

Pukeiti Gardens – walks
A few kilometres south of Oakura is the turnoff to Pukeiti Gardens (11 km from the highway up Upper Pitone Road), the internationally renowned rhododendron garden set amongst rainforest on the edge of Egmont National Park. The 360-ha garden is one of the largest of its type in the world, and its collection of rhododendrons is botanically very significant. Open all year, though October–November is best for rhododendron flowers.

Oakura–Opunake
Beaches beyond Oakura are wilder and more remote and are reached via side roads signposted as you drive through Okato, Puniho, Warea and Pungarehu. A right turn down Bayly Road (just past Warea) takes you to the coast and a loop back to SH 45 before Pungarehu. Parihaka Pa, site of the world's first passive resistance movement against colonial forces (said to have inspired Gandhi) is reached via Parihaka Road signposted ahead of Pungarehu (call 06 763 8708 to visit the pa). Sunset on Mt Taranaki viewed from Cape Egmont Lighthouse, 6 km west of Pungarehu, is another highlight. The curious hillocks either side of the road are the congealed lahars (mudflows) from past eruptions of the omnipresent volcano to the east. At Oaonui is the Maui gas production factory, the onshore facility where gas piped ashore from the South Taranaki Bight is processed.

Opunake – campground, walks
Opunake's Middleton Bay features a clifftop walking track and lookout over the coast. There's a popular beachfront campground and safe swimming from the beach, while the Sugar Juice Café on the main street is the best of the region's travellers' cafés by a long margin.

Kaupokonui and Ohawe Beaches – swimming, beach walks
Both of these popular beaches (signposted before and after Manaia respectively) are worth the diversion off SH 45.

Dawson Falls – walks
Dawson Falls in Egmont National Park is 20 minutes by a good but narrow bush-lined road from Manaia, past the Kapuni natural gas production facility, and Kaponga village (fuel). Dawson Falls has a historic and authentic Swiss chalet-style lodge and

café, DoC's Konini Lodge, a park visitor centre, and a number of short walks and longer excursions on the flanks of Mt Taranaki. Recommended short walks are those to Wilkies Pools and to Dawson Falls (roughly 50 steps down to the base of the falls for the best view).

Hawera

Distinguished by its impressive 1914 water tower, Hawera has many other notable historic buildings (a self-guide brochure on these is available from the visitor centre below the tower), and the widely acclaimed Tawhiti Museum (signposted from the centre of town) – considered one of the country's best private museums (café). One of the museum's displays is a re-creation of the huge Turuturu Mokai Pa, focal point of the nearby historic reserve on Turuturu Road. A good coffee is to be had at The Café on Princes Street, next to the Post Office.

32 New Plymouth–Wanganui SH 3
157 km, 2.5 hours

This is the main touring route south from New Plymouth, across the ringplain formed by Mt Taranaki, and then along coastal plains, dunelands and hill country to Bulls. With numerous towns, small settlements and the city of Wanganui en route, there is no lack of facilities for travellers.

On the outskirts of New Plymouth is the Meeting of the Waters Scenic Reserve, a good place for a picnic, walks in native forest and swimming. Further down the road at Egmont Village (12 km from New Plymouth) is the excellent Kauri Cottage café and the turnoff to North Egmont Visitor Centre in Egmont National Park.

North Egmont, Mt Taranaki – walks

Twenty minutes from Egmont Village, after a narrow, winding but beautiful drive through the forests of Egmont National Park, the road emerges at the bushline at North Egmont. There is an excellent park visitor centre and small café here, several forest and alpine walks and fine views of the surrounds and the North Taranaki coast.

Stratford/East Egmont – walks

Back on SH 3, kids will no doubt enjoy the toy factory at Inglewood (try Macfarlanes café), otherwise it's a straight run through to Stratford, home of New Zealand's first Glockenspiel clock, performing daily at 10.00 a.m., 1.00 p.m. and 3.00 p.m. in the clocktower halfway down the main street. Signposted at the northern end of the town is the Pembroke Road access to East Egmont. The sealed road (access to Manganui Skifield) climbs well beyond the forest edge to the Stratford Plateau (1100 m) for commanding views of the region, coastline and, on a clear day, the central North Island volcanoes. Back down the mountain you will find a small DoC office, forest walks and the Mountain House accommodation and restaurant.

Just south of Stratford is the Taranaki Pioneer Village project, a replica village offering visitors a slice of pioneering history.

Eltham – walks

Eltham, like Hawera (see Route 31), has many historic buildings, some of which are over 100 years old. You can see these for yourself by picking up the Historic Eltham brochure from any of the Taranaki visitor centres and following the self-guided heritage walk. Speciality cheeses produced by the local industry can be tasted and bought from the Cheese Bar at the 'No entry' end of Bridge Street - here's hoping they improve their signage. The busy In Flame café on the main road is the best bet for good refreshments.

Hawera

Three kilometres south of Hawera is the largest dairy factory in the Southern Hemisphere, run by the Kiwi Cooperative Dairy Company. Although you can't tour the factory, the adjacent Dairylands Visitor Centre and museum is surprisingly good value. Taranaki is first and foremost dairying country and Dairylands is the place to learn more about this industry, with its interactive displays, and even a simulated milk tanker ride in a full size model tanker! Kids love it. There's a café here too.

Hawera–Wanganui

Allow an hour between Wanganui and Hawera, a trip which passes through Patea and Waverley and many small country settlements. The drive along coastal plains and hill country is pleasant enough, and Patea's black sand beach is worth visiting for walks, a picnic or to let the kids loose in the playground. Waverley's Big Sun café has been recommended, or try the Mai Mai café/restaurant.

Wanganui

Wanganui is a river city with a rich Maori and European history, particularly in times when the Whanganui River was the main route to the central North Island. The city's regional museum, Virginia Lake on Wanganui's northwestern outskirts, the Sarjeant Art Gallery and Moutoa Gardens on the banks of the Whanganui River provide reasons to take a break here. The attractively restored historic precinct at the river end of Victoria Avenue has a number of good cafés to choose from. Jolt is the best of these (you'll float through the door on the strong coffee aroma), Cracked Pepper the next best, but for something more funky and gluten-free head around the corner to the Red Eye Café on Guyton Street. On Moana Ave is the recommended Left Bank Café. SH 4 (the Parapara road) leads north from Wanganui to Tongariro National Park.

Mt Taranaki

NEW PLYMOUTH

Inglewood

Stratford

SH45 to
New Plymouth

SH43 to
Taumarunui

(3)

Eltham

HAWERA

Lake Rotorangi

atea

NORTH

Waverley

(3)

Waitotara

Waitotara River

Maxwell

New Plymouth–Wanganui SH 3
157 km • 2.5 hours

New Plymouth
▲
35 km
▼
Stratford
▲
32 km
▼
Hawera
▲
28 km
▼
Patea
▲
62 km
▼
Wanganui

Kai Iwi

(3)

Whanganui River

WANGANUI

PALMERSTON NORTH

Manawatu River

Oroua Downs

Himatangi

1

SH3 to
Palmerston North

Sanson

Rangitikei River

SH1 to
Hunterville

Bulls

3

Turakina

Whangehu

Whangehu River

3

WANGANUI

LEVIN

①

FOXTON

Foxton Beach

Manawatu River

Himatangi Beach

NORTH

Wanganui River

33 Wanganui—Wellington SH 3, 1
192 km, 3 hours

The route from Wanganui to Wellington follows SH 3 through farmland as far as Bulls, where it joins SH 1, the main north—south highway. Traffic is noticeably heavier beyond Bulls, particularly at weekends. South of Sanson on the coastal plains between the Rangitikei and Manawatu rivers is the lengthy Foxton straight, notorious for speeding drivers. Highlights include side journeys to beaches at Himatangi, Foxton, Otaki, Waikanae, Paraparaumu and Paekakariki, and several worthwhile museums and galleries. (Note that the route map does not show the Levin—Wellington section of SH 1.)

At Otaki, south of Levin, the beautiful Rangiatea Church on Te Rauparaha Road is a highly recommended and a nationally significant example of Maori craftsmanship and colonial architecture, which has recently been restored after a fire destroyed the original building. Otaki's Bank Heritage Museum and Waikanae's Mahara Gallery regularly hold regional and touring exhibitions, while the entertaining Hyde Park Museum at Te Horo is one of several examples in the area of informal collections of nineteenth- and twentieth-century curios and collectables. Lastly, the Southward Car Museum at Otaihanga is outstanding.

Kapiti Island, just off the Kapiti Coast near Paraparaumu, has been completely cleared of introduced mammals, and is now an important nature reserve with abundant birdlife. It can be accessed for day and overnight trips by water taxis from Paraparaumu Beach (check ahead for schedules, a permit is required from DoC to visit the island).

There are several good cafés on this stretch: recommended are the Mothered Goose at Bulls, the Laughing Fox at Foxton, Brown Sugar at the south end of Otaki, The Front Room at Waikanae Beach, and Café Vella at Plimmerton. Two hundred metres past Café Vella is the waterfront — a very pleasant walk on a sunny day.

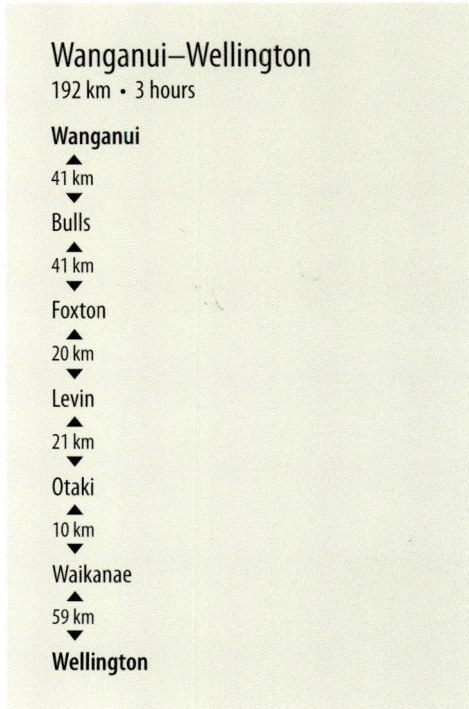

Wanganui—Wellington
192 km · 3 hours

Wanganui
▲
41 km
▼
Bulls
▲
41 km
▼
Foxton
▲
20 km
▼
Levin
▲
21 km
▼
Otaki
▲
10 km
▼
Waikanae
▲
59 km
▼
Wellington

TAUPO

Lake Taupo

Hatepe

1

Waitetoko

Motuoapa

SH41

Turangi

SH46

Lake Rotoaira

Tongariro River

Mt Tongariro

Mt Ngauruhoe

1

Desert Road

Mt Ruapehu

Rangipo Desert

Lake Moawhango

SH49 to Ohakune

Waiouru

Hihitahi

Taupo–Taihape
134 km • 2.5 hours

Taupo
▲
49 km
▼
Turangi
▲
56 km
▼
Waiouru ◀ 27 km ▶ Ohakune
▲
29 km
▼
Taihape

NORTH

34 Taupo–Taihape SH 1
134 km, 2.5 hours

The scenic highlights of this route are provided by the 105-km drive around Lake Taupo and along the Desert Road past the Tongariro volcanoes to Waiouru. Beyond here interest pales unless you've a penchant for rural scenery. SH 1 is the North Island's busiest highway and fuel and refreshments are available at most centres.

Turangi – campground, walks
The drive to Turangi stays close to the lakeshore and there are many beaches, picnic sites and walks (see DoC's *Taupo Walks* brochure) to enjoy. Two spots to mention along the way are Motuoapa with the excellent Licorice Café and a pleasant lakeside area around the yacht marina, and the Waiotaka Scenic Reserve with picnic tables beside the lake (popular with the swans). Turangi has a very good information centre. The best café in town is the excellent Mustard Seed Café, and the legendary hamburgers from Grand Central Fry on Ohuanga Road are worth trying.

SH 47 between Turangi and National Park offers fine views of the Tongariro volcanoes and a number of good short walk opportunities which are covered by a DoC brochure. The Lake Rotopounamu forest walk 11 km from Turangi is recommended for its picnic sites and swimming.

The Desert Road
SH 1 between Turangi and Waiouru involves crossing the Rangipo Desert. The route's outstanding mountain scenery is best experienced in the morning when the volcanoes are lit by the sun. In winter (and sometimes summer) the road can be closed by snowfall.

Waiouru
The Waiouru Army Museum employs audio-visual presentations and static displays of military hardware and photography to recount New Zealand's military history from nineteenth-century land wars to contemporary UN peacekeeping. Far from glorifying the military, the account is often moving. Waiouru's best café is in the museum foyer. If travelling west on SH 49 allow 30 minutes to reach Ohakune. En route you pass the monument to the Tangiwai railway disaster that occurred on Christmas Eve 1953. 151 people were killed when the Wellington to Auckland Express crashed into the Whangaehu River after the rail bridge was swept away by a lahar from Mt Ruapehu.

Taihape
Taihape is the largest centre between Taupo and Bulls, servicing both the local rural and tourist markets. Eating options have improved markedly in recent years – try the Café Exchange and Brown Sugar Café. Taihape's specialist sport is gumboot throwing, and to acknowledge this a huge gumboot has been erected in the main street.

KAIMANAWA
MOUNTAINS

1

TAIHAPE

NORTH

TAIHAPE

Utiku

Mangaweka

1

Ohingaiti

Vinegar Hill

SH54 to
Feilding

Hunterville

1

Rata

Rangitikei River

Marton

1

Feilding

SH3 to
Wanganui

BULLS

Sanson

SH3 to
Palmerston North

SH1 to

35 Taihape–Bulls SH 1
83 km, 1 hour

The drive from Taihape passes through ruggedly beautiful country, with river gorges and high papa cliffs. Seven kilometres south of Taihape is a signposted turnoff to the Mokai Gorge, another spectacular site used in *The Lord of the Rings* movies. Mokai Gravity Canyon operates a kilometre-long flying fox and the highest bungy jump in the North Island, and has a café for you to recover in. Beyond Utiku SH 1 meets the Rangitikei River, one of New Zealand's longest rivers at 185 km, and follows it to Bulls.

Mangaweka, 20 km from Taihape, has an interesting historic main street, and is worth a refreshment stop at the unique Aeroplane Café housed in an elevated DC3 aircraft – you can't miss it! There are also walks here along the old Main Trunk Railway line and tunnels, which were replaced by a deviation in 1981. The new North Rangitikei viaduct nearby is one of the longest and highest in New Zealand.

Five kilometres north of Hunterville, there is a camping ground at Vinegar Hill, located within the Putai Ngahere Reserve on the banks of the Rangitikei River. If you're passing at Christmas or New Year, you'll catch the annual gay and lesbian festival with 'Fashion in the Field' and other events scheduled over the holidays.

Bulls

Bulls, at the junction of SH 1 and SH 3, is well-known for its antique shops and the Ohakea A r Force Museum on the way to Sanson. The town has fun with its name, using quirky signposts (Consta-bull at the police station). The Mothered Goose café/deli right on the busy state highway intersection is the pick of the cafés.

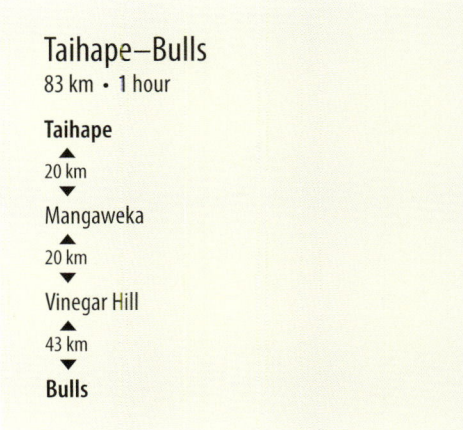

Taihape–Bulls
83 km • 1 hour

Taihape
▲
20 km
▼
Mangaweka
▲
20 km
▼
Vinegar Hill
▲
43 km
▼
Bulls

Rangitikei River

KAINGAROA FOREST

TAUPO

Lake
Taupo

Opepe

Rangitaiki River

Rangitaiki

5

Waipunga River

AHIMANAWA
RANGE

Tarawera

HUIARAU RANGE

Mohaka River

MAUNGAHARURU RANGE

NORTH

TE WAKA RANGE

Te Pohue

5

SH2 to
Gisborne

Esk River

Eskdale

Taupo–Napier
144 km • 2 hours

Taupo
▲
63 km
▼
Tarawera
▲
68 km
▼
Eskdale
▲
13 km
▼
Napier

v

Tutaekuri River

NAPIER

36 Taupo–Napier SH 5, 2
144 km, 2 hours

Once a bush trail used by central North Island Maori and a 2-day stagecoach ride in colonial times, these days the Napier–Taupo highway is entirely sealed and far from the wild ride it was even in the 1960s and 70s. The road crosses rough and remote terrain as it cuts through the Ahimanawa Range and descends from the Volcanic Plateau towards Hawke's Bay.

Seventeen kilometres from Taupo is the start of the Northern Loop track (30–45 minutes) in the Opepe Scenic and Historic Reserve (see DoC's *Taupo Walks* brochure), notable for its remnant of mature forest that has survived volcanic eruptions, fires and logging. Waipunga Falls lookout is 49 km from Taupo in the Waipunga Valley shortly before Tarawera settlement. From the tearooms at Tarawera, a 15-minute track through the bush leads to hot pools that are maintained by the locals.

The route then crosses the Mohaka River, climbs the Maungaharuru Range (very good views of the surrounding country) and descends to the Esk Valley wine growing area, meeting SH 2 at Bay View, 10 minutes north of Napier.

There are tearooms at Tarawera and Te Haroto, and more sophisticated offerings at wineries in the Esk Valley, and towards Napier.

Napier
Napier is regarded as the Art Deco capital of the world. Following a massive earthquake in 1931, fires destroyed most of the commercial heart of Napier. The city was rebuilt with a variety of buildings in the style of that era and by the end of the decade Napier was the newest city on the globe. Napier's Art Deco is unique, with Maori motifs and buildings designed by Louis Hay, admirer of the architect Frank Lloyd Wright. A walk through the city with the Art Deco Trust's leaflet guide is well worthwhile. The Hawke's Bay Museum has a riveting display about the earthquake, which is still New Zealand's worst natural disaster.

Waipunga Falls

Art Deco Rothmans Building, Napier

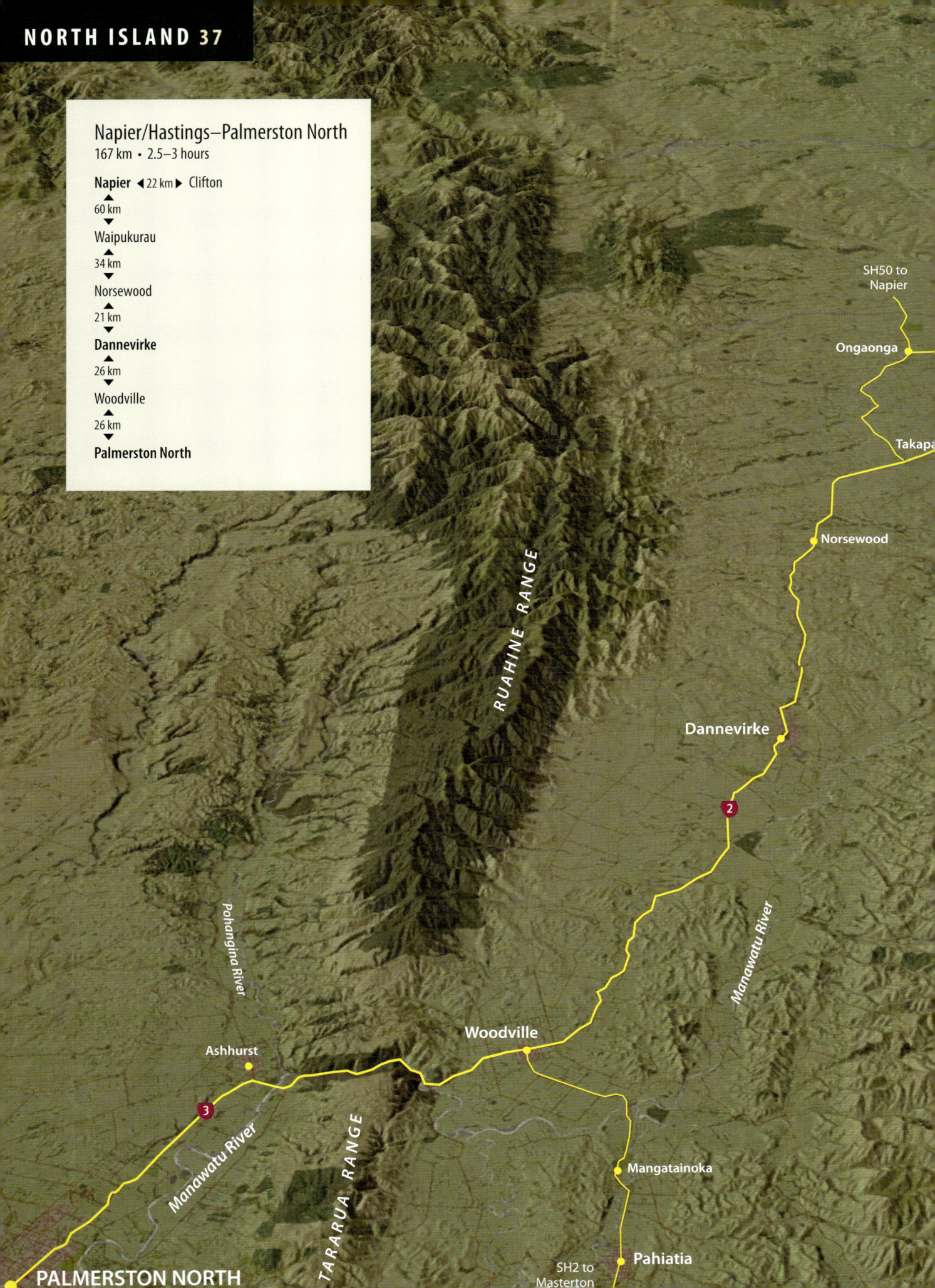

Napier/Hastings–Palmerston North

167 km • 2.5–3 hours

Napier ◀ 22 km ▶ Clifton
▲
60 km
▼
Waipukurau
▲
34 km
▼
Norsewood
▲
21 km
▼
Dannevirke
▲
26 km
▼
Woodville
▲
26 km
▼
Palmerston North

SH50 to Napier

Ongaonga

Takapa

Norsewood

RUAHINE RANGE

Dannevirke

2

Manawatu River

Pohangina River

Woodville

Ashhurst

3

TARARUA RANGE

Manawatu River

Mangatainoka

Pahiatia

SH2 to Masterton

PALMERSTON NORTH

37 Napier/Hastings–Palmerston North SH 2, 3
167 km, 2.5–3 hours

South of Napier and Hastings, SH 2 rolls through the dry country landscapes east of the Ruahine Range. Sheep farming is the major industry, but farm forestry, winemaking and market gardening are prominent too. Locals recommend scenic drives to Te Mata Peak, Ocean Beach and Waimarama southeast of Hastings, and to Porangahau, south of Waipukurau. The most popular diversion, however, is the trip to Cape Kidnappers to observe the gannets.

 Cape Kidnappers Gannet Reserve – campground, walks, picnicking

The Cape Kidnappers Gannet Reserve contains New Zealand's largest colony of Australasian gannets. November to late February is the best time to visit – public access is closed between July and October. To reach the colony turn off SH 2 just beyond Clive (10 km from Napier) and make for the coast at Haumoana and drive on toward Clifton (12 km). Art and craft galleries, wineries and cafés are well established between Haumoana and Clifton (Clifton's Clifton Bay Café is the pick of the eating establishments). The beach walk to the Cape (5 hours return) and most guided tours by vehicle begin at Scotsmans Point just short of Clifton (campground). You need to check the tides before setting out on the walk. An informative DoC brochure is available from visitor centres.

 Waipawa/Waipukurau/Ongaonga

Twenty minutes from Hastings on SH 2 is the excellent Paper Mulberry Café (organic wholefoods and good coffee), while at the south end of Waipukurau is another fine travellers café – Hatuma Café.

Waipawa and Waipukurau are bustling service towns. Waipawa's Settlers Museum is its main attraction, but for a real sense of the region's settler history the diversion west to Ongaonga (on SH 50, 17 km from Waipawa) features numerous preserved historic buildings, 11 of which are listed with the New Zealand Historic Places Trust. (SH 50 between Takapau and Napier is covered by a Heritage Trail brochure.)

 Norsewood/Dannevirke

In 1872 a sailing ship arrived in Napier with several hundred Scandinavian settlers who established the communities now known as Norsewood and Dannevirke, in the hills at the base of the Ruahine Range. Their heritage is preserved in Norsewood's Pioneer Museum, kids' troll trail and the country's smallest cheese factory – Rangiuru Farm – where you can sample and buy from a range of delicious organic cheeses. Twenty kilometres further south, Dannevirke has the best options for feeding the hungry and thirsty: the Black Stump Café on the main street or the Barrelhouse on Ward Street.

 Woodville/Manawatu Gorge – walks

Those that appreciate cheesecake as an essential food group should visit Yummy Mummy's Cheesecake café in Woodville – you'll be in heaven. SH 2 is an easily-missed left turn at the southern end of town but it doesn't matter if you miss the turn as the drive through the Manawatu Gorge towards Palmerston North is worth it. On the hills above the gorge are 55 turbines of the Te Apiti wind farm. The gorge itself has SH 3 clinging to one side while a railway line negotiates the cliffs and tunnels opposite.

From Palmerston North, SH 3 runs north to connect with SH 1 south of Bulls, while travelling south SH 57 connects with SH 1 near Levin.

Feilding

Ashhurst

RUAHINE RANGE

SH3 to
Palmerston North

SH2A
Napie

WOODVILLE

Manawatu River

Mangatainoka

PALMERSTON
NORTH

Manawatu River

Pahiatua

2

Mangatainoka River

T A R A R U A   R A N G E

NORTH

Eketahuna

Mount Bruce
National Wildlife Centre

Mount Bruce

2

Ruamahanga River

Woodville–Masterton
81 km • 1 hour

Woodville
▲
40 km
▼
Eketahuna
▲
15 km
▼
Mt Bruce National Wildlife Centre
▲
26 km
▼
Masterton

to
Castlepoint

MASTERTON

38 Woodville–Masterton SH 2
81 km, 1 hour

Of the two routes to Wellington from Woodville (the other being via Palmerston North, Shannon and Levin on SH 56 or 57, 2.5 hours), this route east of the Tararua Range through Wairarapa's wide river valleys and undulating hill country offers more varied and interesting travelling.

Wairarapa's highlights include the Department of Conservation's National Wildlife Centre at Mount Bruce and rewarding drives to the coast at Castlepoint and Palliser Bay. In southern Wairarapa craft artists, clothes designers, winemakers and restaurateurs have made the most of Wairarapa's proximity to Wellington and established a boutique shopping and café culture that has enlivened Masterton, Featherston, Greytown and Martinborough. The preservation of colonial buildings, especially in Greytown, has done much to enhance the character of these southern towns. You will find a succinct account of the region's Maori and European history in the very good *Heritage Trails of Wairarapa* booklet (free at visitor centres).

Mangatainoka/Pahiatua

Nine kilometres from Woodville, beer boffins will enjoy a tour of Mangatainoka's main attraction, the historic Tui Brewery (tastings included of course). Bookings are required. Further up the Mangatainoka River is Pahiatua, a town that began as a nineteenth-century roading camp in the vast totara forest that once extended between Mount Bruce and Takapau in Central Hawke's Bay. 'Forty Mile Bush', as the tract between Mount Bruce and Woodville was named, was felled from the 1870s by Scandinavian immigrants contracted by the colonial government for their tree-felling and roadbuilding skills. One can only marvel at their thoroughness as you drive south through what has become prosperous sheep and dairy farming country. Pahiatua has the perfectly acceptable Black Stump Café.

Mt Bruce National Wildlife Centre – walks

The largest remnant of Forty Mile Bush occurs 17 km south of Eketahuna at Mount Bruce. Since 1962 this 945-ha reserve has been the home of the Mt Bruce National Wildlife Centre, a captive-rearing facility central to efforts to prevent the extinction of many of New Zealand's endangered birds, including takahe, kokako, stitchbird and the Campbell Island teal. Birds reared here are eventually released on offshore reserves such as Kapiti Island, or back to the wild to bolster struggling populations.

For the public, the centre is an excellent educational facility which utilises displays, videos, and an audio-visual presentation to outline its work and the Department of Conservation's endangered species recovery programmes. Many of the endangered birds can be viewed in specially constructed forest aviaries, while brown kiwi and tuatara are housed in indoor facilities.

Easy walks through the forest of tall totara, rimu, kahikatea and tawa are likely to bring sightings of other more common forest birds. A special treat will be a sighting of North Island kaka (a large forest parrot) which have been successfully released into the forest. Kaka are fed daily at 3 p.m. as part of a supplementary feeding programme. And if you're in need of a supplementary feed yourself, there's a café at the centre. Just south of the Mt Bruce Centre is the Wee Red Barn, selling seasonal local produce including some organic items, strawberries and wines.

Masterton

From Mount Bruce SH 2 crosses a spur that falls from the Tararua Range, then descends the Ruamahanga Valley to Masterton, Wairarapa's main commercial centre. Turn off at the northern end of the town for the drive to Castlepoint (see below). Café options in Masterton include Café Strada (main street) and the excellent Entice Café attached to Aratoi, Wairarapa's regional museum and gallery on Bruce Street. A more elegant dining experience can be found at Café Cecille in the centre of Queen Elizabeth Park.

39 Masterton –Wellington SH 2
95 km, 1.5 hours (see map overleaf)

Allow an hour to reach Wellington from Masterton over the Rimutaka Range. While the highway is narrow in places there are numerous passing lanes. Snow or particularly bad weather can lead to road closures. There are toilets at the top of the range at the Summit Cafe and a passable café at Kaitoke Country Gardens, but it's probably worth carrying on to Petone on the edge of Wellington Harbour where several standout cafés are located on Jackson Street – including the Palace, Caffiend and Go Bang Espresso!

Carterton/Greytown/Featherston – picnicking

Rural decline and loss of key industries have greatly affected these small rural service centres, but Greytown and Featherston have done well by refocusing on the visitor industry and heritage tourism. At Clareville (just before Carterton) you will find the Devine Café, or if you have kids in tow, try the very child-friendly Café Bambino. Carterton's Wild Oats café and bakery is recommended, otherwise push through to Greytown.

The Waiohine Gorge, 10 minutes north of Greytown is a popular recreational and picnicking area. Greytown residents and entrepreneurs have retained the town's colonial character by enhancing its classic wooden Victorian buildings, many of which now house cafés, galleries and antique shops. Papawai Marae occupied an important place in New Zealand's history when it was home to the Kotahitanga (Maori Parliament) movement in the 1890s. The locals really are very spoilt with the Main Street Deli and Café, the French Baker (and café, opposite) and Salute café/restaurant. Last but not least, stock up on chocolate supplies for the South Island at Schoc Chocolate, 1 km south of Greytown's main shopping area.

Featherston, at the base of the Rimutaka Range has, like Greytown, retained many of its Victorian buildings, a number of which have New Zealand Historic Places Trust listings. Along with galleries and cafés (the Lady Featherston café is the pick of them), Featherston's Heritage Museum is well worth a visit.

NORTH

TARARUA RANGE

Waiohine River

MASTERTON

Carte

2

Greytown

Featherston

Rimutaka
Summit

Te Marua

UPPER
HUTT

SH58 tp
Paremata

Hutt River

2

LOWER
HUTT

SH1 tp
Porirua

Wellington Harbour

WELLINGTON

Martinborough

Lake Wairarapa

53

to
Lake Ferry,
Ngawi,
Cape Palliser

RIMUTAKA RANGE

Featherston–Martinborough and Cape Palliser
1 hour

Martinborough

Martinborough is 15 minutes from Featherston via SH 53. Alternatively, you can bypass Featherston by taking a route direct from Greytown (signposted). Martinborough's ascent as a premiere winemaking region has boosted the town's popularity, particularly with weekend visitors from the capital. The Martinborough fairs in February and March draw tens of thousands of people. At other times of the year you can sample the region's wines, in particular its outstanding Pinot Noir, at the Martinborough Wine Centre or at boutique vineyards within walking distance from the town. Medici Café is recommended for lunches or, if you just want a coffee to go, go to the Post Office!

Palliser Bay – campground, walks, swimming, picnicking

The route to the coast at Palliser Bay begins at the Martinborough Square and skirts the Aorangi Range in Haurangi Forest Park. Shortly before Lake Ferry (motorcamp) the route turns toward Whangaimoana. The road winds for a short time above the bay offering views across Cook Strait to the South Island. When the road reaches the coast at Te Kopi look for the start of the track to the Putangirua Pinnacles (2 hours return, camping), an impressive area formed by 'badlands' erosion which featured in *The Return of the King* – the third film in *The Lord of the Rings* trilogy.

Eastern Palliser Bay has a long history of human occupation. There are burial sites all along this coast, while rock walls dating to the twelfth century at Te Humenga Point are among the earliest evidence of Maori settlement in New Zealand. After Te Kopi the road follows the coast to Cape Palliser, much of the way being unsealed. There's a shop at the extraordinary Ngawi fishing village where the fleet is hauled ashore by tractor. Cape Palliser Lighthouse is a short distance from Ngawi and the great slabs of rock called Kupe's Sails – said to be the sails that powered the canoe of Kupe, the Polynesian voyager. Seals from a nearby colony, the largest in the North Island, loll about on the rocks and in tidal pools. There are plenty of places to picnic and enjoy the coastal scenery.

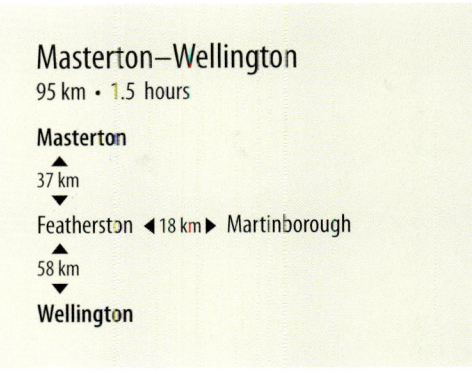

Masterton–Wellington
95 km · 1.5 hours

Masterton
▲
37 km
▼
Featherston ◀ 18 km ▶ Martinborough
▲
58 km
▼
Wellington

NORTH

Pelorus Sound

Kenepuru Sound

Portage

Ngakuta Bay

The Grove

PICTO

Linkwater

Koromiko

Havelock

Queen Charlotte Drive

1

Kaituna River

6

Okaramio

Rapaura

Wairau River

Kaituna

Rapaura Road

Picton–Havelock
64 km • 1 hour

Picton ◀ 35 km ▶ Havelock via Queen Charlotte Dr

▲
23 km
▼

Spring Creek

▲
41 km
▼

Havelock

Renwick

Woodbourne

SH63 to
St Arnaud

40 Picton–Nelson SH 6 & Queen Charlotte Drive
109 km via Queen Charlotte Drive, 1.75 hours
138 km via Blenheim (Rapaura Rd), 1.75 hours

Queen Charlotte Drive is the most scenic route to Nelson, however driving along the Rapaura Road route takes you into the heart of the Marlborough wine growing area. *The Treasured Pathway* (Nikau Press) offers informed coverage of the natural and cultural features experienced along both of these routes.

Picton
Since early times Picton has been a transit point for people and freight between the North and South islands. Today it is also the starting point for kayaking and wildlife adventures around the Marlborough Sounds. The café options have improved substantially in the last few years – try Le Café (overlooking the harbour at the north end of the main street) for quick and easy but decent fare. However, beating Le Café by far is the coffee at Escape to Picton which can be found about 150 metres past Le Café around the corner beside the marina – they offer the regular espresso options plus a tempting menu of special coffees with liqueurs etc. Their food menu is a little different from the norm, and their dessert options are sinful.

Queen Charlotte Drive – campgrounds, walks, swimming, boating
Queen Charlotte Drive begins in Picton (signposted off SH 1). This picturesque 35-km drive links Queen Charlotte and Pelorus sounds before joining SH 6 at Havelock. Narrow and winding at times, the road has several lookouts over the sounds and passes sublime forest-fringed bays with safe beaches and seaside campgrounds. For a leg-stretcher or picnic site, visit Anakiwa (turn right at Linkwater) at the southern end of the Queen Charlotte Walkway. Note that if driving in the other direction, to catch a ferry to Wellington, this route is no faster than driving via Rapaura Road (see below) and may even be slower.

Havelock via Rapaura Road – wineries, fruit stalls
Turning west along Rapaura Road (leave SH 1 about 23 km south of Picton at Spring Creek) is quicker than driving into Blenheim and immediately places you in Marlborough's world famous wine-growing area. In the space of 15 km come numerous wineries – among them Hunters, Nautilus, Cloudy Bay and Allan Scott – offering tastings, wine sales and cafés. Grab a winery guide and map from an information centre. Rapaura Road meets SH 6 to Nelson just before Renwick (tearooms, supermarket, petrol etc). Driving back towards Blenheim offers more wineries and fruit stalls.

Havelock – campground, boating
The fishing village of Havelock, at the head of Pelorus Sound, is now a thriving tourist village with several cafés and curio stores. Try the Mussel Pot if you want to sample the local marine produce. There are several cafés along the main road but follow the signs to the Commercial Wharf for the Slip Inn, overlooking the marina.

Pelorus Sound

French Pass

D'Urville Island

Tennyson Inlet

Croisilles Harbour

Okiwi Bay

Rai Saddle

6

Rai Va

Whangamoa

Delaware Bay

Whangamoa River

Pepin Island

B R Y A N T   R A N G E

Whangamoa Saddle

Hira

6

Wakapuaka

Atawhai

Dun Mount

Nelson Haven

Brooklands

NELSON

Canvastown

Beyond Havelock, where SH 6 crosses the Wakamarina River, is the Trout Hotel at Canvastown. Gold was discovered here in 1860, leading to a brief population boom. The historic Pelorus Hotel remains, renamed the Trout Hotel to reflect more contemporary use of the river, though you can still try your hand at gold-panning.

Pelorus Bridge Scenic Reserve – campground, walks, picnicking, swimming

Twenty kilometres from Havelock, this remnant lowland forest on the banks of the Pelorus River has been a travellers' waypoint for over 100 years. There's a great swimming hole, several short forest walks, and a café/tearoom serving ice-cream and unexciting café food.

Tennyson Inlet/French Pass – campground, swimming

Just beyond Rai Valley a road leads off to the beautiful Tennyson Inlet (1 hour, last few kilometres unsealed from Opouri Saddle) and to French Pass (2 hours, unsealed from Okiwi Bay) in the outer Pelorus Sound. The turbulent water in the French Pass Passage races through on each tide at up to eight knots, creating whirlpools, eddies and fearsome currents. Once navigated by Maori in canoes, it proved more difficult for French seafarer Dumont d'Urville. In 1827 he spent several days investigating the passage and damaged his ship on the way through.

French Pass settlement has a safe swimming beach, picnic areas, a DoC campsite and a garage with essentials and dive tank fills. The variety of wildlife in this area is impressive, and there are several companies offering nature tours, sea kayaking, fishing and diving.

On the other side of the passage lies D'Urville Island, the eighth largest island in New Zealand with an area of approximately 150 square kilometres. Walks and some accommodation are available on the island, which can be accessed from French Pass.

Continuing on SH 6, the road crosses the Rai and Whangamoa saddles, a landscape dominated by the region's pine plantation forests. At the bottom of the winding descent from the Whangamoa Saddle, just past Hira, is the turnoff to Cable Bay. A narrow 11-km road leads to a fine swimming bay with a small campground and the Cable Bay Café. The bay takes its name from the deep-sea telegraph cable which was brought ashore from Sydney in 1876, completing the 15,757-mile link from Britain to New Zealand.

Beyond Hira, the road crests a hill to reveal wonderful views across Tasman Bay to the Abel Tasman coastline and the mountains of Kahurangi National Park.

Havelock–Nelson
74 km • 45 minutes

Havelock
▲
19 km
▼
Pelorus
▲
9 km
▼
Rai Valley
▲
46 km
▼
Nelson

Tasman Bay

SH60 to
Takaka

Riwaka

MOTUEKA

Port Motueka

Tasman

Lower
Moutere

60

Ruby Bay

Motueka River

Ngatimoti

Upper
Moutere

Woodstock

Stanley Brook

Tapawera

GOLDEN DOWNS

FOREST

Kohatu

Nelson–Motueka
48 km • 45 minutes

Nelson
▲
14 km
▼
Richmond
▲
17 km
▼
Mapua
▲
17 km
▼
Motueka ◄ 58 km ► Kohatu Junction

SH6 to
Kawatiri
Junction

Motueka River

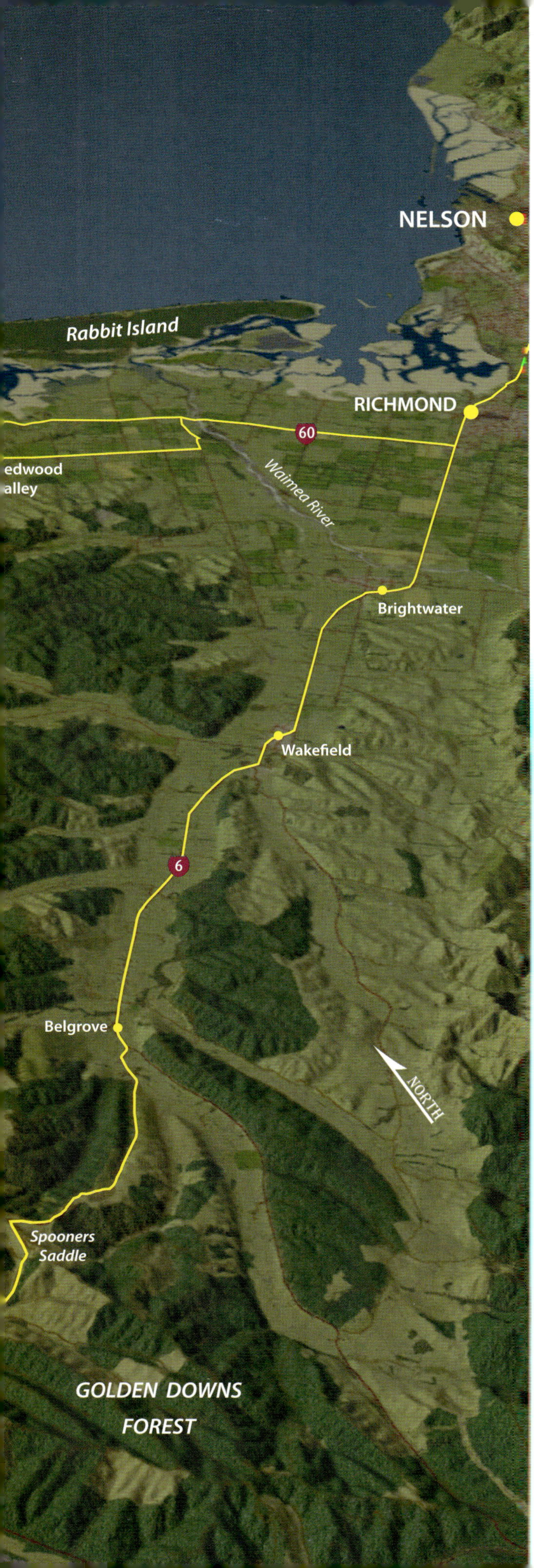

NELSON

Rabbit Island

RICHMOND

60

Waimea River

edwood alley

Brightwater

Wakefield

6

Belgrove

NORTH

Spooners Saddle

GOLDEN DOWNS

FOREST

41 Nelson—Farewell Spit SH 6, 60

154 km. 2.5 hours

This drive combines all that makes a visit to Nelson and Golden Bay so memorable — beaches, mountain scenery and forest walks, craft galleries, wineries and cafes. A regional art guide, *Art in Its Own Place* will greatly enhance the journey across the Waimea Plains, over Takaka Hill's marble landscape, and into the quieter recesses of Golden Bay. Pamphlets are available on the walks noted below from information centres.

Nelson/ Richmond and environs

Nelson city brims with cafés and restaurants. Highly recommended are Hopgoods, Bar Delicious, Broccoli Row and the Suter Gallery Café (by the Queens Gardens) in the central city, or The Boatshed on the waterfront. Continuing south on SH 6 you soon reach Stoke, location of the World of WearableArt (WoW) Gallery — the must-visit centre of the internationally renowned Montana WoW Awards Show. There is a good café here, and the classic car museum next door is also a popular attraction.

Richmond is 14 km south of Nelson on SH 6 on the edge of Waimea Estuary and the Waimea Plains. SH 60 turns toward Motueka and Golden Bay at a roundabout south of Richmond. Between Richmond and Mapua are numerous wineries, cafés and craft galleries (all well signposted, but grab a handy local map), notably Waimea Estate's Café in the Vineyard, Seifried Estate winery and Silkwood Arts and Crafts. Redwood Road, 6 km from Richmond, leads to Rabbit Island, one of the region's best beaches.

Tahunanui Beach, Nelson

Mapua/Ruby Bay/Tasman

SH 60 allows glimpses of Waimea Estuary as you travel toward Mapua – a pleasant seaside hamlet at the mouth of Waimea Estuary which has several cafés, including the long established Smokehouse Café. Try also the Naked Bun bakery and café for their sophisticated take on pastries (their custard squares are phenomenal), cakes and breads, or Hamish's for ice-creams – a must for liquorice lovers. Mapua's aquarium is small, but highly recommended for the kids.

Ruby Bay has Dido's for takeaway or eat-in curry and pizza, and a couple of excellent winery cafés nearby, including Ruby Bay Wines. Tasman's Jester House café, with its spacious garden, playground and tame eels, has long been a family favourite, and the food is great too.

Motueka – campground

After Tasman and the drive around Moutere Inlet you reach Motueka (45 minutes from Nelson). A decent coffee can be found together with local and organic produce at the Toad Hall store (at the southern end of town). For a good café meal try the Arcadia Organic Café in the main shopping area. Motueka's swimming beach and salt water baths are on Wharf Road (turn right at the roundabout on the southern edge of the town).

Richmond–Motueka via the Moutere Highway

This alternative inland route, with views of the Mt Arthur Range, is sometimes quicker than the busier SH 60. It turns off SH 60 just past the Waimea River bridge. Kahurangi Winery Café is located just before Upper Moutere, while Neudorf Vineyard is located north of Upper Moutere village – take a picnic, buy a bottle of their wine and enjoy the vineyard setting. The excellent Riverside Café is on the outskirts of Motueka at Lower Moutere.

42 Motueka–Kohatu Junction SH 61
58 km, 1 hour (see map previous page)

A useful shortcut to SH 6 for those travelling from Golden Bay to the Lewis Pass and Christchurch. The road follows the eastern flanks of Kahurangi National Park along the Motueka River, an outstanding trout fishing river. To access the park, turn off at Ngatimoti for the Mt Arthur road end, and at Tapawera for the Wangapeka Track. Both access roads are unsealed. Tapawera is the largest locality on SH 61, with a garage and store.

Totaranui Beach, Abel Tasman National Park

41 Motueka–Golden Bay SH 61
57 km, 1 hour (see map overleaf)

After Motueka, SH 60 crosses the Motueka River and leads toward Abel Tasman National Park and Takaka Hill. Real fruit ice-cream and organic fruit can be bought from roadside stalls. Shortly after Riwaka village, roads lead from SH 60 around the coast to Kaiteriteri Beach or over the hill to Marahau.

Kaiteriteri/Marahau (Abel Tasman National Park) – campground, walks, picnicking, swimming, kayaking

Marahau, 20 minutes from the SH 60 turnoff, is at the southern entrance to Abel Tasman National Park and is the base for sea kayaking, launch tours and day walks in the park. The park's renowned beaches and coastal forests can be sampled on Tinline Walk and the return trip to Coquille Bay (both 1 hour), but don't expect solitude. There are now two cafés here, including Hooked on Marahau, down by the beach, and Park Café at the start of the Abel Tasman coastal track.

Kaiteriteri is a very busy little place in summertime – which is not surprising with such a beautiful beach and sheltered bay. Several cafés, a store and campground look after visitors.

Takaka Hill – walks, views

The summit of Takaka Hill is a fascinating landscape of water-etched marble outcrops, sinkholes and caves. Though it is a slow, winding grind to the top (prone to slips in bad weather, with ice and occasional snow in winter) there are several rewarding walks and viewpoints over Tasman and Golden bays. These include the source of the Riwaka River (at the base of the hill, where the river emerges from a cave); Hawke's Lookout, a short walk from SH 60 close to the summit; and the walk to Harwoods Hole – a spectacular 176-metre shaft – which begins 15 km down Canaan Road (signposted) in Abel Tasman National Park. Take care on the narrow gravel road, and allow 1.5 hours for the walk. Before SH 60 descends to the Takaka Valley is the new Takaka Hill Walkway (2–3 hours) and Harwood Lookout with outstanding views of Kahurangi National Park.

Upper Takaka/Cobb Valley – campground, walks, picnicking

A left turn at Upper Takaka leads up the Takaka River to the Cobb Power Station, and thereafter up a steep unsealed road to the Cobb Reservoir where there are several interesting day walk possibilities onto the Peel Range or to Lake Sylvester. Allow 1 hour to the reservoir. The road is often narrow and winding, and not recommended for campervans.

Takaka – campground

Just before Takaka is Paynes Ford Scenic Reserve, a top rock climbing area, though it's the swimming hole here that attracts most people. Takaka (1 hour from Motueka) in high summer is the vibrant centre of Golden Bay, with its craft outlets, weekend market and eateries. The Wholemeal Café is an excellent Takaka institution but several good new places can also be recommended – the Dangerous Kitchen, Brigands and Eatery on the Rocks (on the Nelson side of Takaka in pleasant garden surrounds). Newly established is Schnapp Dragon, found down the lane beside Wholemeal Café, featuring local products including liqueurs, mead, cheese, wine, olive oil and salami. Inland from Takaka is the Anatoki Salmon Farm where you can have some fun catching your own salmon. You only pay for what you catch, and the staff will prepare and hot-smoke it for you to eat there or take away.

Takaka–Totaranui (Abel Tasman National Park) – campground, walks, swimming, fishing

Totaranui is 32 km (1 hour) from Takaka. The road passes Pohara Beach (campground, beach) where one of Golden Bay's newest and best cafés is found – the Totally Roasted Coffee House and Roastery. From Wainui Bay the road is unsealed (suitable for campervans) as it climbs over a forested range to Totaranui. Apart from the fine beach here, there is a DoC visitor centre, campground and walks toward Awaroa or Anapai bays.

Te Waikoropupu Springs/Pupu Walkway – walks

Back on SH 60, 4 km west of Takaka is the turnoff (at the Waitapu Bridge) to these renowned and quite beautiful springs – the clearest fresh water in the Southern Hemisphere. An easy forest walk past old gold diggings leads to the springs. The springs are sacred to Maori and swimming in them is considered a desecration of their mauri or lifeforce. The Pupu Walkway (2 hours return through mature podocarp forest) is reached via a gravelled road to the springs.

Wharariki Beach, Golden Bay

NORTH

Wharariki Beach

Cape Farewell

Port Puponga

Whanganui Inlet

Pakawau

Paturau River

Ruatahuna Inlet

Aorere River

Collingwood

Parapara Inlet

Onekaka

60

Ligar B'

Tarakohe

Te Waikoropupu Springs

TAKAKA

Pohara

Paynes Ford

Harwoods Hole

Takaka River

Uruwhenua

60

Canaan Road

Riwaka ●
"Resurgence"

Upper
Takaka

Cobb
Reservoir

Motueka–Farewell Spit

106 km • 1.75 hours

Motueka
▲
35 km
▼
Upper Takaka
▲
22 km
▼
Takaka ◀32 km▶ Totaranui
▲
27 km
▼
Collingwood
▲
22 km
▼
Puponga

Farewell Spit

Anapai
Bay

Totaranui

Awaroa
Inlet

Awaroa

ABEL TASMAN
NATIONAL PARK

Marahau

Sandy Bay

Kaiteriteri

Riwaka

Motueka River

MOTUEKA

SH60 to Nelson

Collingwood – campground, swimming

Between Takaka and Collingwood (27 km) SH 60 stays inland until Parapara Inlet, with viewpoints overlooking Golden Bay, the Abel Tasman coastline and Farewell Spit. There are some quality crafts to be found along this route including fine pottery and paintings at Estuary Arts. Expect good hospitality and food at the Mussel Inn country café and brewery at Onekaka (presenting the tail of a dead stoat or feral cat will earn you a free beer as an incentive to reduce introduced pests). Otherwise, the Naked Possum is a great little place whose menu features wild game. Collingwood, at the mouth of the Aorere River, is where you organise tours to the Farewell Spit bird sanctuary or transport to the Heaphy Track, and enjoy good food and coffee at the Courthouse Café. For more treats, visit Rosy Glow Chocolates on the beachfront.

Pakawau – campground

From Collingwood SH 60 skirts Ruataniwha Inlet and returns to the coast at Totara Avenue where signs warn the motorist to watch for penguins crossing the road. The road follows a long sweep of beach to Pakawau where there is a popular campground and the Old School Café. Just past Pakawau a road leads to Whanganui Inlet and Paturau River mouth on the west coast (32 km) – a five-star scenic drive, unsealed.

Puponga/Farewell Spit/Wharariki Beach – walks, picnicking

Farewell Spit Visitor Centre and the Paddlecrab Café are located a short distance from Puponga on a rise overlooking the spit's high wind-whipped dunelands. Easy walking tracks lead from the centre across Puponga Farm Park to the spit's outer and inner coastlines. The (half-day) clifftop walk toward Wharariki Beach is one of the best in Golden Bay, though the shorter walk to Fossil Point is also rewarded with outstanding scenery.

A 10-minute drive north of Puponga leads to a carpark and 20-minute walk across grassy dunes to the beautiful Wharariki Beach – for many the highlight of a visit to Golden Bay. You can take long walks down the beach, and watch seals in the surf off the spectacular Archway Islands. The track towards Farewell Spit climbs high onto cliffs and within view of seal haul-out zones and nursery areas.

Farewell Spit, Golden Bay

43 Nelson–Westport SH 6
226 km, 4 hours

Allow a day to enjoy this drive to the West Coast. Highlights are the crossing of Hope Saddle and the journey through the forested scenic reserves and earthquake-riven landscapes of the Buller Gorge. SH 6 also provides access to Nelson Lakes National Park.

Nelson–Kawatiri Junction – views, picnicking
Quick progress is made south of Nelson city past Richmond and several small rural centres to Belgrove. Past here SH 6 climbs to the crest of the Spooners Range in the heart of the vast Golden Downs pine plantation. (NB: The road that departs Belgrove through Golden Downs Forest to St Arnaud is the fastest route to Nelson Lakes from Nelson city. Allow 1 hour.) SH 6 meets SH 61 from Motueka at Kohatu Junction (see Route 42), and thereafter continues up the Motupiko Valley toward Hope Saddle – where there are superb views of Nelson Lakes and the Kahurangi mountains. The Buller River is reached at Kawatiri Junction (picnicking and short walks). SH 63 turns here for St Arnaud (25 km) and Blenheim (127 km, 1.5 hours).

Murchison
From Kawatiri Junction the route closely follows the Buller River as it descends toward Murchison through beech forest reserves and farmed river flats. At Gowanbridge, 6 km from the junction, is the access road (sealed) to Lake Rotoroa. Near Murchison it is worth pausing for the views back toward the grey marble flanks of Mt Owen. Murchison's Commercial Hotel has a café with great coffee and cake. The Murchison Museum is worth a look if you have time.

Inangahua
Beyond Murchison the Buller enters a forested gorge with impressive rapids and huge earthquake slips. SH 6 crosses the Buller at O'Sullivans Bridge 11 km from Murchison. A few minutes further on is the somewhat contrived 'swingbridge' attraction. Save your energy for free beech forest walks at Lyell, the site of a nineteenth-century mining town (camping, picnicking and historic relics). At the Inangahua Hall, residents have established a fine historic display that recounts the tremendous earthquakes that devastated the Inangahua/Murchison area in 1928 and 1967.

Lower Buller Gorge–Westport
The slow and graceful passage of the Buller between banks of rata forest is a superb finale to this drive as it traces the lower gorge toward Westport. If you look across the river you can see the route of the old railway line, now no longer in use though it will probably make an enjoyable bike trail some day.

Tasman Bay

NELSON

Wakefield

Spooners Saddle

Belgrove

Kohatu

Motupiko

GOLDEN DOWNS FOREST

6

Hope Saddle

Mt Owen

SH63 to St Arnaud

Kawatiri Junction

Gowanbridge

Lake Rotoroa

TASMAN MOUNTAINS

Owen River

6

Murchison

O'Sullivans Bridge

SH65 to Springs Junction

LYELL RANGE

Lyell

BRUNNER RANGE

6

Inangahua

MOUNT WILLIAM RANGE

Berlins

Lower Buller Gorge

6

Ohikanui River

Nelson–Westport

226 km • 4 hours

Nelson

▲
54 km
▼

Kohatu Junction

▲
39 km
▼

Kawatiri Junction ◄ 25 km ► St Arnaud

▲
35 km
▼

Murchison

▲
52 km
▼

Inangahua Junction

▲
46 km
▼

Westport

44 Westport–Karamea SH 67
97 km, 1.5–2 hours

Though it's usually less than two hours to Karamea, you can easily spend a day pottering around historic coal-mining settlements, and enjoying walks and coastal and forest scenery along the way. Terry Sumner's *Buller Walks* (Nikau Press) is an excellent guide to this area. DoC brochures are also available.

Denniston – views, walk
Denniston is a former coal-mining town on the Denniston Plateau, 8 km above Waimangaroa. The plateau has a stark beauty and it offers fine vistas over the coast when the weather allows. Dotted around the place are mine relics and historic buildings; the Denniston Walkway between Waimangaroa and Denniston takes 3–4 hours one way.

Granity/Ngakawau – walks
After a relaxing break at Granity's Drifters Café you can drive up the hill and walk around the old Millerton township and mine. Otherwise, three kilometres from Granity at Ngakawau is the rewarding Charming Creek Walkway which follows an old railway route through river and gorge scenery.

Mokihinui – campground
SH 67 turns inland at Mokihinui on the Mokihinui River mouth. Just over the river bridge, a left turn and short drive leads to a West Coast institution – the Cow Shed Café with its adjacent accommodation complex and coastal scenery.

Karamea Bluff Ecological Reserve
The scenic highlight of the route to Karamea is the climb up the Radiant Range through the Karamea Bluff Ecological Reserve's outstanding podocarp forest, which will be ablaze with flowering rata in summer. At the base of Taffytown Hill the highway returns to coastal plains at Little Wanganui.

Karamea – campground
Karamea is the last stop before the Heaphy Track, 15 km away at Kohaihai in Kahurangi National Park. The 2 hour return walk along the Heaphy to Scotts Beach offers a taste of this beautiful forested coastline. One of New Zealand's most rewarding short walks is that to the 43 m high Oparara limestone arch in the forests of the upper Oparara Valley (turn off (signposted) 8 km from Karamea and follow the unsealed road over a steep saddle to a carpark).

Top Arch, Oparara River, Kahurangi National Park

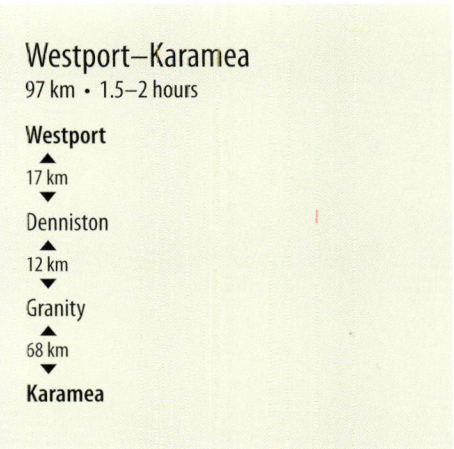

Westport–Karamea
97 km • 1.5–2 hours

Westport
▲
17 km
▼
Denniston
▲
12 km
▼
Granity
▲
68 km
▼
Karamea

Beach north of Karamea

SH6 to Murchison

Inangahua Junction

WESTPORT

Cape Foulwind

Carters Beach

6 Buller River

Tauranga Bay

69

Charleston

Reefto

Reefton Saddle

6

Woodpecker Bay

7

Wa

Punakaiki

Ikamatua

Dolomite Pt

Little Grey River

Totara Flat

P A P A R O A   R A N G E

Ahaura River

Barrytown

Ahaura

Blackball

Grey River (Mawheranui)

Ngahere

6

NORTH

Rapahoe

Runanga

Stillwater

7

Arnold River

GREYMOUTH

Lake Brunner (Moana)

Westport–Greymouth
101 km • 1.5–2 hours

Westport ◄79 km► Reefton

26 km   44 km
▼   ▼

Charleston   Springs Junction

31 km
▼

Punakaiki

20 km
▼

Barrytown

24 km
▼

Greymouth

45 Westport–Greymouth SH 6
101 km, 1.5–2 hours

The Cape Foulwind seal colony, Paparoa National Park's superb coastal scenery, and probably the only place in New Zealand where you can tuck into a buffalo meat hamburger – all within 101 km. This is another drive with enough to easily fill a day. Keep an eye out for cyclists on the narrower tracts around the coast.

Cape Foulwind seal colony – walks

The walkway to the New Zealand fur seal colony at Cape Foulwind is one of the best on the Coast. I'd recommend the 15-minute interpreted walk to the colony from the Tauranga Bay end, which is reached from Westport along SH 67a past Carters Beach and the Cape. The full walkway requires 1.5 hours one way. Back at Tauranga Bay is the superb Bay House Café. There's a direct route back to SH 6 down Wilson's Lead Road.

Charleston – campground, walks

Views of the Buckland Peaks on the northern Paparoa Range dominate the views inland towards Charleston, another West Coast mining town well past its glory days. The short walk to the Charleston sea cliffs or along the beach from the Nile River mouth are enjoyable diversions, and you can learn much about the harshness of settler life by walking round the old Charleston cemetery above the Nile River.

Fox River – walks, swimming

After Charleston the road turns inland for a stretch before returning to the coast and the languorous sweep of Woodpecker Bay, where limestone cliffs loom over the beach near the Fox River at the northern boundary of Paparoa National Park. The walk up the Fox River leads to the Fox River caves (3 hours return) and canyon (5 hours). Otherwise at low tide you can explore tidal platforms toward Seal Island.

Punakaiki – campground, walks

The drive to Punakaiki, over cliffs and headlands below spectacular limestone bluffs and coastal forest, is superb. Trumans Track, 2.5 km before Punakaiki, is a highly recommended short walk at low tide by cliffs, caves and rock pools. It's hard to avoid the crush of tourists at Punakaiki if you arrive in the middle of the day in the tourist season, but the pancake rocks and blowholes at Dolomite Point in a sou'westerly swell are always exhilarating. The best coffee and food here is at Punakaiki Crafts.

Barrytown Flats – walks, buffalos

Interspersed amongst the farmland on Barrytown Flats are remnant groves of nikau palms and lush coastal forest. At Pakiroa Beach, down the road past the Barrytown pub, fossickers occasionally turn up greenstone amongst the shingle. Of the Coast's quirky attractions, none is more so than the sight of East Asian buffalos on the hill south of the pub. No ploughs or loincloth-clad farmers here – these beasts are being fattened to be turned by the chefs at the Rata Café into steaks, burgers and casseroles. There are plenty of other eating options for the buffalo-averse.

Past Barrytown SH 6 resumes its cliff-side convolutions to Greymouth, past wind-beaten forest, glimpses up narrow canyons and hazy views over coastal headlands and the sea.

46 Westport–Greymouth via Reefton (Grey Valley) SH 6, 69, 7
158 km, 2.5 hours

The inland route to Greymouth traverses the eastern flanks of the Paparoa Range, down the Grey Valley from Reefton to the coast. It also connects travellers with SH 7, the quickest route between Westport and Christchurch.

The drive between Westport and Inangahua (44 km) is a wonderful drive up the lower Buller gorge with forest scenery, graceful river bends and wide shingly rapids. At Inangahua Junction, 1 km from Inangahua, go straight ahead down the Inangahua Valley (SH 69), between the Paparoa and Victoria ranges along farmed river terraces to Reefton (34 km).

Reefton – campground, walks

Highlights of a visit here are the area's historic goldmining sites, buildings and forest walks. First stop in Reefton should be at the very good Reefton Visitor Centre on Broadway. Some of the best walks are those from SH 7 between Reefton and Springs Junction (see below). Reefton's Reef Café is the pick of the cafés in this area by a long way.

Reefton–Greymouth, 79 km

From Reefton SH 7 crosses Reefton Saddle and descends to the Grey Valley's south bank. An interesting side trip is to the site of the abandoned Waiuta mine and village (signposted 23 km from Reefton, 8 km unsealed, brochure and on-site interpretation). Otherwise, you might cross the Grey at Ikamatua and drive to Blackball, visit the famous historic 'Hilton' Hotel or stock up on locally made salami. Blackball is at the start of the Croesus Track across the Paparoa Range. Back on the south bank, the route to Lake Brunner and to Jacksons on SH 73 (Arthur's Pass) turns off at Stillwater. On the way to Moana is the historic Arnold River power station site (forest walks), while the Stationhouse Café at Moana on the shores of Lake Brunner offers brunch, lunch, a kids' menu and anything from muffins to gourmet burgers and a la carte dining in the evenings.

SH6 to
Westport

Buller River

O'Sullivans Bridge

MURCHISON

Lake Rotor...

Shenandoah

65

Maruia River

Marble Hill

Springs
Junction

Maruia
Springs

SH7 to
Reefton

7

Lewis Pass

M A I N   D I V I D E   O F   T H E   S O U T H E R N   A L P S

Lewis River

NORTH

Nina River

Boyle River

Boyle Village

...tful River

Lewis River

Windy
Point

7

SH7
Culverd...

Hope River

Murchison–Lewis Pass

104 km • 2 hours

Murchison
▲
83 km
▼

Springs Junction
▲
15 km
▼

Maruia Springs
▲
6 km
▼

Lewis Pass

47 Murchison–Christchurch via Lewis Pass SH 65, 7, 1
292 km, 4 hours (see maps this page and overleaf)

Of the three crossings of the Alps (the others being Arthur's and Haast passes), the Lewis is easiest to drive thanks to the comparatively gentle approach up its western side. The first leg of this journey follows the Maruia Valley to its headwaters at Lewis Pass, with fine mountain scenery and corridors of upland beech in the Lewis Pass National Reserve. It then descends to the Waiau River to eventually emerge on the Amuri Plain near Culverden, and joins SH 1 at Waipara. Highlights of the drive are thermal resorts at Hanmer and Maruia Springs, forest walks in the reserve, and a rare opportunity to stand astride one of Planet Earth's continental plate boundaries.

Murchison
Murchison (see Nelson–Westport, Route 43 for more information) is on the Buller River which is followed for 11 km to O'Sullivans Bridge. Here, SH 6 to Westport crosses the bridge, and SH 65 continues ahead towards the confluence of the Buller and Maruia rivers. Between here and Springs Junction (allow an hour) the highway shadows the Victoria Range on the western side of the valley's farmed river flats, and ranges flanking the main Southern Alps chain to the east.

Maruia Falls – picnicking
This 9-metre waterfall 22 km from Murchison was formed by the Murchison earthquake in 1929. Remarkably, the fall was originally about 1 metre, but has grown 8 metres as the riverbed below has lowered. The relatively safe runout has made running the falls popular with kayakers.

SH 65 continues up the Maruia Valley until a gorge section forces a deviation up the Shenandoah River and around Mt Rutland. The road narrows beyond Ruffe Creek and requires care in the forested gorge before the climb to Shenandoah Saddle. Beyond the saddle the route rejoins the Maruia, following wide farmed river flats to Springs Junction.

Springs Junction
SH 65 ends at Springs Junction where it meets SH 7 between Greymouth and Waipara (allow 45 minutes to cross Rahu Saddle to Reefton, see Westport–Greymouth, Route 45 for details). If you like white-bread sandwiches and chips with everything then the café at Springs Junction is the place for you, and some people have experienced good coffee there too.

Marble Hill Scenic Reserve – campground, picnicking
In the grassy paddock next to this innocuous little reserve, about 7 km toward Lewis Pass, the edge of the Pacific continental plate is grinding past the Indo–Australasian plate, forcing the Southern Alps skywards and skewing the West Coast northwards. Honest! This boundary, also called the Alpine Fault, runs up the western side of the Alps from Milford Sound to Nelson Lakes. Here at Marble Hill the scene of the action is a boggy terrace running across the paddock where in 1964 geologists placed a concrete wall at right angles to the fault to measure any movement. On the upper side of the terrace is the Pacific Plate, on the lower side the Indo–Australasian. It is rare in the world to find an exact and active surface expression of a major plate boundary. It may distress some to learn that Richter 8 earthquakes along the Alpine Fault are believed to have occurred every 300 years, and one of these is well overdue. On the plus side, proximity to the fault is responsible for the thermal springs that lie ahead.

Maruia Springs – walks
From Marble Hill the road winds through beech forest next to the gravelly upper reaches of the Maruia River. About 2 km before Maruia Springs is the easy Waterfall Track (20 minutes return). Maruia Springs resort (98 km from Murchison) has public and private pools – the hot water is piped from the springs on the north bank of the river.

Lewis Pass – walks, picnicking, views
Lewis Pass is about 5 km beyond the resort after a steep climb through forest with views north toward Gloriana Peak. Just below the pass on the Canterbury side is a carpark at the start of the St James Walkway, a nice picnic spot amid alpine scenery and forests. There is a nature trail around the nearby alpine wetland, or a longer walk down to the picturesque Cannibal Gorge (2 hours return), where centuries ago Ngai Tahu warriors were said to have overwhelmed a party of Ngati Wairangi, and killed and eaten them – but don't let that put you off your lunch.

Maruia Springs

Banks Peninsula

CHRISTCHURCH

Waimakariri River

Pegasus Bay

Kaiapoi

Woodend

Rangiora

Ashley River

Amberley

Waipara

SH1 to
Kaikoura

Weka Pass

Waikari

Harwarden

Hurunui

Hurunui River

BALMORAL FOREST

AMURI PLAIN

Culverden

SH70 to
Waiau

Red Post Corner

ORGAN RANGE

Waiau River

HANMER PLAIN

HANMER SPRINGS

Lewis Pass–Christchurch
188 km • 2.5 hours

Lewis Pass
▲
62 km
▼
Hanmer Junction ◀ 10 km ▶ Hanmer Springs
▲
27 km
▼
Culverden
▲
41 km
▼
Waipara
▲
58 km
▼
Christchurch

NORTH

WYE RANGE

POPLARS RANGE

Hope River   7

Lewis Pass–Hanmer Springs

The turnoff to Hanmer Springs is 62 km from Lewis Pass, the first 20 km of which follows the Lewis River south through corridors of beech toward the Boyle River (where the highway turns east). Now on open and scrubby farmed river terraces flanked by high ranges, the road crosses to the southern bank of the river and joins the larger braided Waiau River, generally staying high above it until the junction with SH 7a.

Hanmer Springs – campground, walks

Hanmer Springs is an alpine spa town which has been frequented by tourists since the 1860s. The main attraction, the town's outdoor thermal reserve, is a lovely place for a soothing soak. Hanmer has a range of cafés and bars – try the Springs Deli Café for food, and The Powerhouse Café for the best coffee. There are many short walks in the Hanmer Forest, which is predominantly comprised of introduced conifers – forest trails are also popular with mountain-bikers. In winter the Amuri Skifield adds another attraction to the town's list of outdoor activities. The drive up Jacks Pass (unsealed) takes you to the edge of the high country between Hanmer and Blenheim. Acheron Accommodation House, a cob cottage built in the 1860s, now a registered historic place, is a short distance from the pass in the Clarence Valley. It is possible to drive through Molesworth Station to the Awatere Valley south of Blenheim during summer - find out exactly when by contacting information centres in Hanmer or Blenheim (see Picton–Christchurch, Routes 52 and 53 for details).

Culverden/Hurunui – campground

From Hanmer Springs SH 7 continues along the Waiau Valley through rolling hills to emerge on the Amuri Plain. Here the highway leaves the river and turns south toward Culverden. SH 70 to Waiau and the inland route to Kaikoura turns off just before Culverden (see Kaikoura–Christchurch, Route 53). If you've skipped Hanmer you can get good quality café fare at Culverden's Red Post Café. Otherwise you can find genuine rabbit and ostrich pies at the historic Hurunui Hotel 13 km further past the Balmoral pine plantation (campground), just over the Hurunui River. Waipara and the SH 1 junction is 28 km away. See Route 53 for information on cafés between Waipara and Christchurch.

Culverden

Fox Glacier

SH6 to
Fox Glacier

Whataroa

Poerua River

Harihari

Wanganui River

Mt One One

Pukekura

Lake
Ianthe

Waitaha River

Ross

Mikonui River

Ruatapu

Hokitika River

road to
Lake Kaniere

HOKITIKA

NORTH

Arahura River

6

Kumara

SH73 to
Arthur's Pass

Kumara Junction

Taramakau River

Greymouth–Fox Glacier
201 km • 3.5–4 hours

Greymouth
▲
40 km
▼
Hokitika ◀ 19 km ▶ Lake Kaniere
▲
27 km
▼
Ross
▲
46 km
▼
Harihari ◀ 20 km ▶ Wanganui River mouth
▲
30 km
▼
Whataroa ◀ 13 km ▶ Okarito
▲
33 km
▼
Franz Josef
▲
25 km
▼
Fox Glacier

Shantytown

Gladstone

6

Peter Ridge

Karoro

GREYMOUTH

Grey River (Mawherau

48 Greymouth–Fox Glacier SH 6

201 km, 3.5–4 hours (see maps this page and overleaf)

Much of this memorable journey into South Westland is within sight of the high peaks of the Southern Alps. Even when it's wet (and it does rain at times!), the wild coastline, rainforests, lakes, rivers and glaciated landscapes are no less extraordinary. By Whataroa you will have entered Tai Poutini/Westland National Park and the northern reaches of the vast Te Wahipounamu South-West New Zealand World Heritage Area. Some words of advice: take insect repellent and buy fuel at Greymouth or Hokitika – prices at places like Whataroa and Franz Josef amount to daylight robbery. West Coast wild food – including whitebait and venison – are specialities worth looking out for in the region's cafés, and every March Hokitika hosts the famous Wild Foods Festival.

Greymouth – campground, walks

Greymouth, a good place to gather information about the journey south, is not short of attractions itself. They include quality coffee from the Smelting House Café on MacKay Street or DP1 Squared (yes, it's a café) on Mawhera Quay (by the Grey River floodwall); quality food from Café 124 on Mackay Street; quality beer (and brewery tour) at Monteiths Brewery; and Shantytown, a model nineteenth-century mining village 13 km south of the town. Greymouth has a number of short forest walks within the borough – covered by a DoC brochure. On dolphin-watching boat cruises, you're likely to see fur seals and coastal birds as well as the critically endangered Hector's dolphin.

Hokitika – campground, walks, picnicking, swimming, boating

Hokitika is about 30 minutes south of Greymouth and 15 minutes from the SH 73 junction (Arthur's Pass and Christchurch). The town's attractions include its jade/craft galleries and one of the Coast's best museums. Café de Paris is the pick of the cafés, along with Café Priya for those after a decent curry. Nineteen kilometres east of Hokitika is Lake Kaniere where an easy track along its western shores leads through the beautiful podocarp forest that lines the lake's tranquil bays. The full walk requires 4 hours one way, but shorter walks are no less rewarding. Lake Mahinapua is 10 km south of Hokitika on SH 6. There are several short walks and the 2-hour (one way) Mahinapua Walkway, but it's pleasant enough just to fetch up on the lakeshore for a picnic or to camp.

Ross – walks, picnicking

Ross is the centre of the Ross Historic Goldfields, and trails like the water-race walk radiate away from the visitor centre on Aylmer Street. The pride of Ross, which no-one dares criticise within earshot of the locals, is its not-so-historic opencast gold mine a few metres behind the visitor centre – the largest opencast alluvial mine in the Southern Hemisphere.

Pukekura/Lake Ianthe – campground, picnicking, walks

South of Ross, the highway traverses corridors of rimu and matai forest in the Kakapotahi and Waitaha Scenic Reserves. Up the hill from the Waitaha River bridge at Pukekura is the Puke Pub and Wild Food Restaurant, which boasts possum pie and other local delicacies on its menu. Across the road is the quaint Bushman's Centre dedicated to the bushman's arts. Lake Ianthe is a large forest-fringed glacial lake, popular with swimmers, campers and anglers. Natural history tours of the lake by boat leave every half hour.

Harihari – campground, walks, picnicking

From Lake Ianthe SH 6 turns in and toward the foothills of the Southern Alps. The 20-km side trip from Harihari to the Wanganui River mouth leads to one of the lesser-known gems on the coast – the 45-minute walk to the Mt One One (Doughboy) lookout where superb views unfold across unbroken forest to the Alps. You can continue along the coast on the Harihari Coastal Walk to the Poerua River mouth. The Mt One One–Poerua circuit (3 hours) is described in a brochure available at Harihari.

Whataroa

Tours of the white heron colony at Whataroa's Waitangiroto Lagoon are the major attraction. The prominent peak seen from several places between Whataroa and Franz Josef is Elie De Beaumont (3109 m).

Okarito Lagoon – walks, picnicking

A couple of kilometres past Lake Wahapo is the 13-km road to Okarito, a small community of baches and homes on a magnificent stretch of coast bordering Tai Poutini/Westland National Park. Okarito's rimu forests are a symbol of the successful battle against loggers in the 1980s. Their addition to the national park has protected intact a sequence of ecosystems from coast to mountains – rare not just in New Zealand but in the world. Since then it's been learned that the Okarito brown kiwi is a distinct sub-species – recent government funding has established a kiwi sanctuary here. On a fine day the view from Okarito Trig (1.5 hours return) across Okarito Forest to the high peaks of the national park is incomparable. Bird-watching by hired canoe on Okarito Lagoon and beach walks are other popular activities.

Lake Mapourika – campground, fishing, picnicking, boating, swimming

Lake Mapourika, 11 km from Franz Josef is the largest and most scenic of South Westland's glacial lakes. Like the much larger 'great lakes' east of the Alps, these lakes were created as glaciers retreated when the last Ice Age waned 10,000–13,000 years ago.

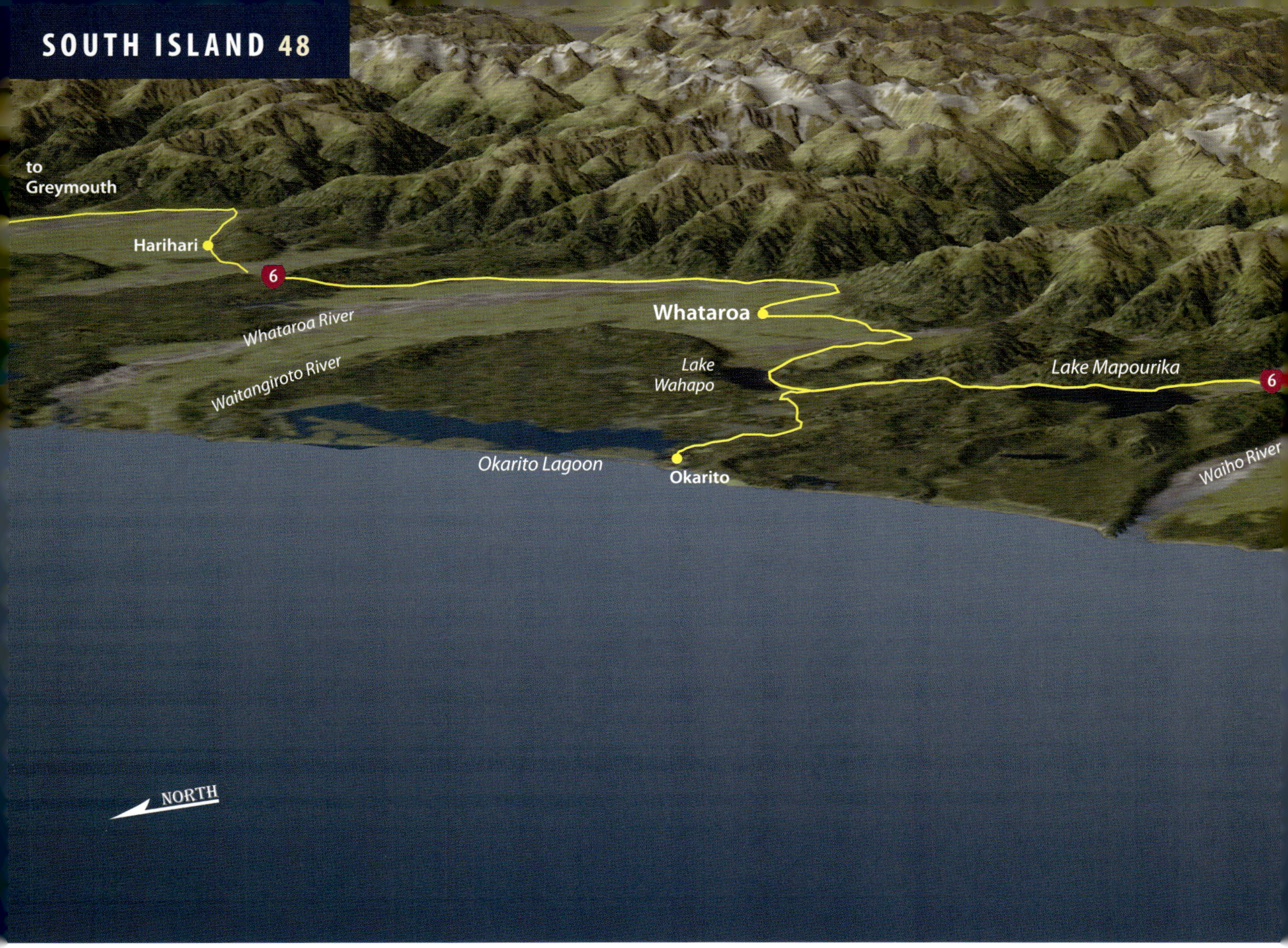

to
Greymouth

Harihari

6

Whataroa River

Waitangiroto River

Whataroa

Lake
Wahapo

Lake Mapourika

6

Okarito Lagoon

Okarito

Waiho River

NORTH

Franz Josef – campground, walks

Franz Josef Glacier has been a tourist icon since the late nineteenth century, and tourists come still in ever increasing numbers to see it. Take your hat, coat and sensible shoes (and earplugs if you're averse to aircraft noise) for the walk to the base of the glacier (1.5 hours return), which begins up the Waiho Valley just south of the village. Be especially careful not to go too close to the unstable terminal face of the glacier. A road-end kiosk within sight of the glacier has an informative series of interpretive panels on glacier formation and the story of the Franz. Guided walks onto the glacier can be arranged at the village. Other high quality shorter walks in the valley include those to Peters Pool, Lake Wombat and to Sentinel Rock – the latter offering good views of the glacier. Information on these walks is found at the DoC visitor centre at the Tai Poutini/Westland National Park headquarters. Alice May Restaurant has the best atmosphere and service.

Fox Glacier – campground, walks

The 25-minute drive to Fox Glacier covers steep forested terrain as it crosses Cook Saddle. Fox Glacier village isn't as developed as Franz Josef, though even that status is changing rapidly. For walkers, access to the glacier is easier and quicker (1 hour return)

than the Franz, and it benefits too from the long established company Alpine Guides Westland whose guides and guided walks enjoy a good reputation. The Fox Glacier terminal is no less dangerous than the Franz. Fox's most regarded walk is the easy circuit through the forests around Lake Matheson (reached off Cook Flat Road toward the coast), famous for its reflections of the Southern Alps at dawn and dusk. When evening light colours the mountains, Gillespies Beach, 19 km from Fox Glacier through Waikukupa Forest (unsealed), is a wonderful place to be.

Sheep farm near Fox Glacier

Mt Elie De Beaumont

Aoraki / Mt Cook

SOUTHERN ALPS (KA TIRITIRI O TE MOANA)

Franz Josef

Omoeroa
Saddle

Cook
Saddle

Fox Glacier

Lake Matheson

6

Cook River

to
Haast

Gillespies Beach

Franz Josef Glacier

FOX GLACIER

Gillespies Beach

Cook River

Karangarua

Karangarua River

6

Jacobs River

Makawhio River

Bruce Bay Bruce Bay

Mahitahi River

Aoraki / Mt Cook

Copland River (hot springs)

Paringa River

Lake Paringa

Lake Paringa

Monro Beach

Lake Moeraki

Moeraki River

Knights Point

M A T A K E T A K E   R A N G E

Ship Creek

NORTH

Haast River

6

Mosquito Hill

HAAST

49 Fox Glacier–Haast SH 6
118 km, 2 hours

The drive between Fox Glacier and Wanaka is dominated by the coastal, forest and mountain landscapes that form the central portion of the Te Wahipounamu South-West New Zealand World Heritage Area. From Haast, the road jags inland for the crossing of Haast Pass to Otago's gentler, beech-forested landscape and the shores of Lake Wanaka. Highlights of the route are the many short walks to a variety of coastal and forest features, perfect for the traveller. Although described as a southward journey below, the best experience of it in my opinion is travelling northwards from Wanaka, leaving around 2 p.m. and driving as the late afternoon and evening sun lights the high peaks and forests between Haast and Fox.

Fox Glacier–Bruce Bay – walks, picnicking

The 46-km drive to Bruce Bay crosses the coastal plains formed by the Cook and Karangarua rivers. Single-lane suspension bridges carry you across these two large fast-flowing rivers – the latter, 30 minutes from Fox, provides access to the Copland Track to Welcome Flat Hut and its nearby hot springs (6–8 hours one way). Bruce Bay, littered with driftwood and lined to the north by rimu forest and ranks of flax, marks a brief return to the coast before the highway again enters forests up the Mahitahi River. Views inland from here reach toward the remote peaks and snowfields of the Hooker–Landsborough Wilderness Area.

Paringa – campground, picnicking

The route between Bruce Bay and Lake Moeraki stays inland, wending through tall dark South Westland forests much of the way. At the Paringa River the route opens briefly onto river plains. On the northern bank is the Salmon Farm and Café. Lake Paringa is enclosed by forest and is a popular swimming, camping and picnicking area.

Lake Moeraki/Monro Beach – walks, picnicking

Just past Lake Moeraki and close to the Lake Moeraki Wilderness Lodge is the forest track to Monro Beach and the Whakapohai Wildlife Refuge (40 minutes one way). The refuge protects breeding areas used by tawaki (Fiordland crested penguin) between July and December.

Knights Point lookout/ Ship Creek – views, picnicking, walks

Four kilometres past Lake Moeraki SH 6 reaches the spectacular coastline north of Haast at Knights Point. After winding around steep headlands and gullies, the road returns to forested coastal plains and a series of dune ridges. At Ship Creek , where the sailing ship *Schomberg* washed up in 1855, is an excellent 20-minute kahikatea swamp forest walk – primeval scenery which has made photographers and film-makers wealthy and is the delight of ecologists who regard this area's forests as the best representation anywhere of the Mesozoic-era swamp forests that existed 100 million years ago. Ship Creek's 30-minute Dune Lake circuit through wind-stunted

forest offers fine views over lake and coastline. The sandflies can be ferocious here – be sure to take repellent!

Haast

Haast is heralded by the crossing of the wide and braided Haast River on the longest single-lane bridge in New Zealand. Inside the Haast Visitor Centre is information on the World Heritage Area and brochures on the walks noted in this section. Haast is the last place for fuel until Makarora (81 km) on the Otago side of Haast Pass. There are a couple of cafés and taverns at Haast township, plus a small supermarket. See below for the Haast–Jacksons Bay description.

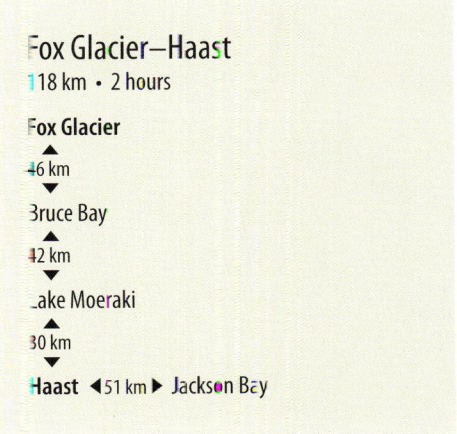

Fox Glacier–Haast
118 km · 2 hours

Fox Glacier
▲
46 km
▼
Bruce Bay
▲
42 km
▼
Lake Moeraki
▲
30 km
▼
Haast ◀ 51 km ▶ Jackson Bay

Bruce Bay, South Westland

Landsborough
River

Fantail Falls

Thunder Creek Falls

"Gates of Haast"

Pleasant Flat

6

SH6
Haast Pa

MATAKETAKE RANGE

SH6 to
Fox Glacier

6

HAAST

Okuru River

Turnbull River

Hapuka
Estuary

Okuru

**Hannahs
Clearing**

Waiatoto River

Waiatoto

HAAST RANGE

NORTH

Arawhata River

Jackson River

Jackson Bay

Neils Beach

Lake Ellery

Jackson Bay

Smoothwater Bay

**road to
Martyr Saddle**

50 Haast–Jackson Bay
51 km, 45 minutes

The short stretch of highway to Jackson Bay, along the coastal strip west of Mount Aspiring National Park, leads to remote beaches and rivers as well as forest and mountain scenery and several interesting walks.

Hapuka Estuary Walk – walk
Just past Okuru is this easy 20-minute walk through coastal forest and the Hapuka Estuary intertidal zone. It is one of those rare places in the world where wetlands are given due for the important ecological role they play. Forest and coastal birds are likely to be seen, while information panels provide natural history interpretation.

Jackson Bay – walks
From Hannah's Clearing the road enters a beautiful corridor of forest, emerging briefly where it crosses the Waiatoto and enters the Haast tokoeka sanctuary. At the legendary Arawata River the sealed route turns west to Ne Is Beach where a bumpy sandy road ends to the Arawata mouth, and a wild beach – watch for penguins! At Jackson Bay a DoC shelter and information kiosk opposite the wharf describes both the natural and cultural history of the Bay, and you can enjoy great takeaways from a restored railway carriage called The Craypot. Walks from here lead to Wharekai Te Kau wildlife refuge (20 minutes, information panels) and Smoothwater Bay (3–4 hours return).

Red Hills Lookout – views
A 22-km unsealed route from just past the Arawata River bridge leads to a lookout over the Cascade River and rugged surrounding hinterland. A lookout (with natural history information panels 3 km past Martyr Saddle offers views south over the valley toward the Red Hills – a region of outstanding natural and wilderness values.

Hapuka Estuary walk

SH6 to
Haast ,
West Coast

Mt Brewster

Blue River

Haast Pass

6

Makarora River

Makarora

Wilkin River

The Neck

NORTH

Lake Hawea

Lake
Hawea

Clutha River

Lake Wanaka

Albert Town

Glendhu Bay

WANAKA

51 Haast – Wanaka via Haast Pass SH 6
142 km, 2.5 hours

Haast River
The way to Haast Pass follows the Haast River to its headwaters, probably the most dramatic of any of the road crossings of the Alps. SH 6 traces the south bank of the river beneath alpine tops and steep forested valley walls on the boundary of Mount Aspiring National Park. Where the Landsborough River joins the Haast, about 40 km from the coast, the Haast River and SH 6 make an abrupt turn south.

Pleasant Flat – campground, picnicking
Located a few kilometres from the Haast–Landsborough confluence, on a fine day Pleasant Flat is indeed pleasant. Vistas spread north up the Landsborough and Clarke valleys to the impressive southern face of Mt Hooker and peaks of the Hooker Range – the centrepiece of the Hooker–Landsborough Wilderness Area.

Haast River

Gates of Haast – views, walks
After Pleasant Flat, the highway crosses the Haast River and enters Mount Aspiring National Park. It's worth stopping for the short forest walk to Thunder Creek Falls. SH 6 then passes the breathtaking Gates of Haast, a narrow and dramatic gorge where slips and enormous boulders choke the river's passage. It is hard to imagine that the easy flowing river a few kilometres on is the source of this imbroglio that cuts steeply down toward the coast. A little further on is another rewarding forest walk to Fantail Falls.

Haast Pass (563 m)
West of the pass the forests are dominated by kamahi, but on the pass itself, atop a gentle rise above the headwaters of the Haast River, silver beech is the most common tree. The Haast is the lowest of the three Southern Alps passes, and, as an interpretive panel notes, it was a well-known route used by Maori. The pass was first reached by a European explorer, J.H. Baker, in 1861 but was then controversially named after Julius von Haast who crossed it to the West Coast in 1863. A packhorse trail over the pass was established by the 1870s, but construction of the highway between Hawea and Haast was spread across no less than 36 years between 1929 and 1965!

Haast Pass–Makarora – campground, walks, picnicking
From the pass you are soon into gentler topography at the head of the Makarora Valley. Towards Lake Wanaka the highway follows the bed of the steadily broadening valley formed by one of many gargantuan glaciers that flowed through the area during the Pleistocene Ice Age. There are camping/picnic sites and walks at Cameron and Davis flats, and a 30-minute walk to beautiful river pools at the mouth of the Blue River. At Makarora there is a DoC visitor centre, campground, store and café.

Lakes Wanaka & Hawea
Most of the 61-km drive between Makarora and Wanaka is high above these impressive glacier-formed lakes. There are a number of lookouts and picnicking sites where you can enjoy lake and mountain scenery, including the camping area at Boundary Creek. See Christchurch–Wanaka, Route 62 for information about services at Wanaka.

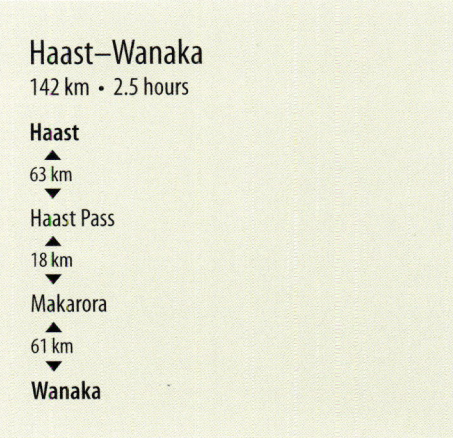

Haast–Wanaka
142 km • 2.5 hours

Haast
▲
63 km
▼
Haast Pass
▲
18 km
▼
Makarora
▲
61 km
▼
Wanaka

Lake Hawea

PICTON

1

Tuamarina

BLENHEIM

Wairau River

SH6 to
Nelson

Awatere River

Seddon

1

*Lake
Grassmere*

*Cape
Campbell*

Ward

Waima River

Tapuae o-Uenuku

IN:LAND KAIKOURA RANGE

Kekerengu

NORTH

Clarence

Clarence River

Waipapa Bay

Ohau Point

SEAWARD KAIKOURA RANGE

Mangamaunu

Hapuku River

1

KAIKOURA

*Kaikoura
Peninsula*

52 Picton–Kaikoura SH 1
160 km, 2.5 hours

SH 1 is the busy main route south to Christchurch. Beginning in Marlborough's world-class wine-growing region, SH 1 passes along Kaikoura's famed whale, dolphin and seal-watching coast before crossing to the Canterbury Plains.

Picton – campground
The Picton Visitor Centre, on the waterfront a few hundred metres from the ferry terminal, is a useful place to collect information on the places ahead. See Picton–Nelson, Route 40 for other information.

Blenheim – campground
Blenheim was one of New Zealand's earliest settlements, its current prosperity founded on the region's suitability for sheep farming and horticulture. These days its fame as a wine-growing region has encouraged an attractive café, wine and craft-trail culture (grab a winery map, and see also Picton–Nelson, Route 40) that draws people from all over the globe. (Take SH 63 up the Wairau Valley to reach St Arnaud and Nelson Lakes National Park – 127 km, 1.5 hours.)

Seddon/Ward – campground, views
Just south of Blenheim is the large Montana winery, after which SH 1 crosses Dashwood Pass to Seddon in the Awatere Valley. From here the vistas west are filled by the foothills rising toward Mt Tapuae-o-Uenuku (2885 m) and its outriders on the Inland Kaikoura Range. (See also the Molesworth Road description below.) Seddon has a couple of cafés including the Oak Tree Cottage tea and coffee shop at the Vavasour winery (turn towards the coast at the Awatere Valley Road intersection before the road/rail bridge).

Kekerengu and Kaikoura Coast – campground
The first leg of the Kaikoura Coast highway to Clarence River lies between steep hillsides and a 30-km shingle beach. Halfway down the beach at Kekerengu is 'The Store' (named after its humble predecessor), a fine café, craft shop and gardens. Best of all is the uninterrupted sea view from the porch while you're enjoying coffee and cake.

At the Clarence River you're confronted by the eastern wall of the Seaward Kaikoura Range, which rises an incredible 2500 metres in just 12 km from the sea – a steeper rise than most of the Southern Alps. Further inland are the southeastern faces of the Inland Kaikoura peaks. Maungamanu Bay is popular with surfers – watch you don't bowl them over as they cross the road. Freshly cooked crayfish are sold from roadside caravans on the rocky coast at the base of the range. There's a DoC campground at Waipapa Bay, and a lookout over the Ohau Point seal colony which is well worth stopping to view.

Kaikoura – campground, walks, marine mammal watching
Kai means food, koura means crayfish; however it's watching ocean mammals that has transformed Kaikoura from crayfishing port to tourist mecca. Once you've recovered your land legs, enjoy lunch at one of Kaikoura's many cafés (Hislop's for organic tucker), or the small mobile eatery serving freshly caught and cooked scallops, mussels and other fishy snacks. You'll then be ready for the circuit or a shorter walk on Kaikoura Peninsula with its seal colonies, birdlife, and great views of the Kaikoura mountains and coast. DoC has done a good job with the displays and information on Kaikoura's natural and human history at the town's visitor centre on the waterfront.

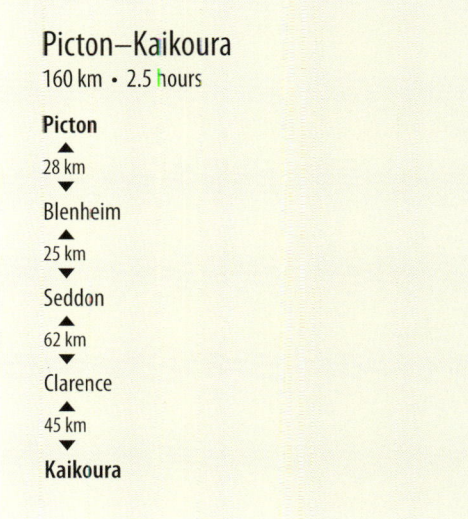

Picton–Kaikoura
160 km • 2.5 hours

Picton
▲
28 km
▼
Blenheim
▲
25 km
▼
Seddon
▲
62 km
▼
Clarence
▲
45 km
▼
Kaikoura

Kaikoura sunrise

53 Kaikoura–Christchurch SH 1
186 km, 2.5 – 3 hours

Cheviot – picnicking
South of Kaikoura at Oaro the road climbs through rural hill country as it crosses the Hundalee Hills to the Conway River. Just before Cheviot, St Anne's lagoon is a nice little bird refuge and picnic spot. Gore Bay, 15 minutes east of Cheviot, is a popular surf beach with safe swimming, picnic sites and a campground. There's no shop. Cheviot has a couple of tearooms, but the best food and coffee is at the very new and nice Two Rivers Gallery Café. Otherwise, continue south 6 km to Domett's Mainline Station – a railway station converted into a pretty good café.

Waipara
SH 1 descends to the Canterbury Plains down the Greta Valley. Waipara is at the junction with SH 7 from Lewis Pass and Hanmer Springs. Several wineries have opened cafés here (Waipara Springs, Mudhouse, Pegasus Bay), while every Sunday from January to the end of March the Weka Pass steam train excursion departs at 11.30 a.m. and 2 p.m. (for the remainder of the year the train runs on the first and third Sundays of the month).

Kaikoura – Waipara via Waiau SH 70, 7
118 km, 2 hours

This is a scenic alternate route to Waipara with fine views of the Seaward Kaikoura and Amuri ranges and back towards Mt Tapuae-o-Uenuku. SH 70 strikes inland 4 km south of Kaikoura and, contrary to current maps, the road is now entirely sealed. Mt Lyford Lodge at the turnoff to Mt Lyford skifield has a good restaurant catering for passing travellers.

Waiau
Waiau is a sleepy village with a store, garage and a couple of pubs. The Ramshead Café and Bar (more bar than café) makes nice scones but head for Hanmer or to Culverden's Red Post Café for a break. SH 7 is 19 km from Waiau, and Hanmer Springs 52 km.

Allow 45 minutes to an hour to reach central Christchurch from Waipara. Three excellent cafés are worth noting – Nor'wester Café in Amberley, Brew Moon Café and Brewery just south of Amberley, and the Pukeko Junction Café just south of Leithfield. Those travelling to Arthur's Pass can turn off at Woodend and travel via Oxford to reach SH 73 at Waddington (58 km). (See Woodend–Geraldine, Route 56.)

Waikari

BALMORAL FOREST

7

Culverden

SH7 to
Lewis Pass

AMURI PLAIN

Waiau River

Waiau

Mt Lyford
Skifield

Whales Back
Saddle

Charwell River

Kaikoura–Christchurch
186 km • 2.5–3 hours

Kaikoura ◀118 km▶ Waipara via Waiau
▲
70 km
▼
Cheviot
▲
58 km
▼
Waipara
▲
58 km
▼
Christchurch

Wairau River

Awatere River

Ward Pass

Molesworth Homestead

Isolated Saddle

RACHEL RANGE

Guide River

Tarndale

Acheron River

Clarence River

Acheron Accommodation House

Clarence River

Jollies Pass

Jacks Pass

HANMER

INLAND KAIKOURA RANGE

Clarence River

NORTH

54 Hanmer–SH 1 via the Molesworth Road
176 km, 5 hours

Two passes immediately north of Hanmer lead into the upper Clarence Valley and to Molesworth Station, New Zealand's largest farm. Between Hanmer Springs and the upper Awatere the road is unsealed but usually passable to all vehicles. Jollies Pass was crossed in 1852 by Edward Lee and Edward Jollie with 1800 sheep, opening the inland route for Canterbury runs to be stocked with sheep from the Wairau. The better road now crosses Jacks Pass.

Molesworth Station evokes New Zealand's high-country identity – musterers, stockmen and their dogs working livestock in vast tussock landscapes. For Maori, the area was an easy summer route to the West Coast by way of the Upper Wairau or Awatere valleys, Tarndale and Lake Tennyson. From the 1850s the main inland route between Nelson/Marlborough and North Canterbury ran through the heart of Molesworth, and the old cob accommodation houses at Tophouse, Rainbow, Tarndale and Acheron are reminders of this. The stock routes never subsequently became public roads and throughout most of the twentieth century the vast majority of New Zealanders were unaware of Molesworth Station.

Molesworth Station today is managed by the Crown, through the Department of Conservation. It is an amalgamation of four separate pastoral leases – Molesworth, Tarndale, St Helens and Dillon – which had been overgrazed by sheep and rabbits and repeatedly burned. With careful management, soils and vegetation have been gradually restored to good health, and up to 10,000 cattle now graze on the land.

The Molesworth Road is opened each summer for a limited season by DoC, usually between New Year and early February. The area's dry-country landscapes are often stunning, especially in the Acheron Valley and the upper Awatere Valley as it rounds the Inland Kaikoura Range. There are no facilities and travellers are advised to be well-prepared for breakdowns, flat tyres etc. There is a fee to use the road. Camping is possible at each end, but not within the station itself. The road is closed during high fire risk periods or bad weather. A brochure about the route is available from visitor centres.

Molesworth Road

Banks Peninsula
97 km • 1.5 hours

Christchurch
▲
▼ 68 km
Little River
▲
▼ 16 km
Duvauchelle
▲
▼ 13 km
Akaroa

NORTH

Le Bons Bay

Okains Bay

Akar

Duvauchelle

Barrys Bay

Hilltop

75

Pigeon Bay

oa Bay

Port Levy

Lyttelton Harbour

Sumner

Evans Pass

Lyttelton

Diamond Harbour

Charteris Bay

Governors Bay

Gebbies Pass

Dyers Pass

PORT HILLS

SH75 to Christchurch

CHRISTCHURCH

Taitapu

Halswell

Prebbleton

Lincoln

55 Banks Peninsula
Christchurch–Akaroa via Port Hills & SH 75
97 km, 1.5 hours

This rewarding scenic route to Akaroa on Banks Peninsula begins on the Summit Road on Christchurch's Port Hills. The return journey can be made via the peninsula's remote harbours and bays on its northern coastline – in total an enjoyable day excursion from Christchurch.

Summit Road
Drive to Sumner village (ice-cream shop and café), then follow your nose up the valley to find the Evans Pass Road. A left turn at the pass takes you to Godley Head (walks, views), and a right turn puts you on the Summit Road, which follows the crest of the Port Hills to Gebbies Pass (1 hour). Exceptional views across Lyttelton Harbour and the Canterbury Plains can be experienced from a number of walks and viewpoints en route. You'll also come across two historic walking houses – the Sign of the Kiwi (now a café) and the Sign of the Bellbird (disused). The road is narrow and must be shared with cyclists, runners and walkers.

Little River
SH 75 is joined below Gebbies Pass at the very good Blue Duck Café. The highway skirts the shallow Lake Ellesmere and turns northeast towards Lake Forsyth and Little River village. The popular Little River Café offers great coffee and lunches, and has a very interesting gallery of contemporary artworks for sale.

Barrys Bay/Duvauchelle – campground, swimming, fishing
From Little River the road climbs to a saddle below French Hill with views over Akaroa Harbour from the Hilltop Tavern (and café). On reaching the cabbage tree-lined harbour at Barrys Bay you can buy locally made cheeses, or turn right and drive 3 km to French Farm winery, now offering a fancy lunch menu as well as winetasting and sales. Heading towards Akaroa you next encounter Duvauchelle village where the Duvauchelle Store and Bistro presents a good menu, or try the old Post and Telegraph office for home-cooked fare, a lot of which is organic. Both have views down the harbour.

Akaroa – campground, swimming, fishing, marine mammals
Historic homes nestle amid the new at Akaroa, which markets its French heritage to the hilt. European architecture, cafés, wine bars, galleries and craft shops lend a relaxed Mediterranean air to the settlement.

A recommended return journey to Christchurch is along the Summit Road above Akaroa back to the saddle at the Hilltop Tavern. From Akaroa take Long Bay Road (past Akaroa Winery and Café) and turn left onto the Summit Road. As well as offering fine views, the road provides access to Le Bons, Okains, Little Akaloa and Pigeon bays. There's a serviced motor camp at Le Bons Bay, and a museum, shop and fuel at Okains. The road between Pigeon Bay and Port Levy is unsealed in places and recommended only for 4WD vehicles.

Lyttelton–Diamond Harbour/Purau Bay/Port Levy – swimming, campgrounds
This route rounds Lyttelton Harbour (café at Governors Bay), passes Charteris Bay (good swimming beach) to reach Diamond Harbour (Godley House Café and gardens). A sealed road (narrow and windy) continues to Purau Bay (swimming beach) and on to Port Levy (12 km from Diamond Harbour).

WOODEND

RANGIORA

Ashley River

Cust

CANTERBURY PLAINS

Oxford

Waimakariri River

Kirwee

Darfield

SH73 to
Christchurch

Waddington

SH77 to
Darfield

Sheffield

SH73 to
Arthur's Pass

Homebush

Glentunnel

Hororata

77

NORTH

Glenroy

Windwhistle

Rak...

77

*Rakaia
Gorge*

Woodend–Rakaia Gorge
100 km • 1 hour

Woodend

▲
39 km
▼

Oxford

▲
19 km
▼

Waddington

▲
42 km
▼

Raikaia Gorge

56 Woodend–Geraldine SH 72, 79

179 km, 2.5 hours (see maps this page and overleaf)

SH 72, the 'Inland Scenic Route', bypasses Christchurch on a route tracing the western edge of the Canterbury Plains. It's also a convenient bypass to SH 73 (Arthur's Pass) for those travelling from Picton, and a less busy route to Mount Cook. Highlights are the Rakaia Gorge, Mt Hutt and the Peel and Alford forests.

Woodend–SH 73 Junction at Waddington

Like much of this route, the 30-minute drive to Waddington via Rangiora and Oxford townships traverses the flat expanses of the Canterbury Plains. There's no danger of starving along here: the small village of Cust has the quiet Route 72 Café, while Oxford is spoilt with a good menu at Café 51 and the unique Jo Seagar's Cook School and Café (Jo Seagar is a well-known New Zealand chef). At the SH 73 junction at Waddington, turn east down SH 73 for about 1 km to return to the Inland Scenic Route.

Rakaia Gorge – campground, walks, fishing

The countryside hereabouts is a mix of sheep farms, forests and market gardens set against the backdrop of rising hills towards Mt Hutt. Glentunnel and Windwhistle are quiet country localities each with a store and a garage. Not far from Windwhistle the route drops sharply into the Rakaia Valley just below the Rakaia Gorge. Jetboating and salmon fishing on this large glacial river are popular activities, as is walking the gorge walkway (3–4 hours return).

The Rakaia River is one of the world's best examples of a braided river. The numerous shallow channels in the gravel-beds appear easy to ford, but when in flood the flow is swift, and many people have been swept away while trying to cross. Early European settlers referred to drowning in rivers as 'the New Zealand death'. Today, jetboating and salmon fishing are more popular activities, along with walking the Rakaia Gorge Walkway. This walkway takes 3–4 hours return, and offers several unique features of geological and historic interest. It starts from State Highway 72 on the northern side of the Rakaia River, upstream of the Rakaia Gorge Bridge.

North Canterbury

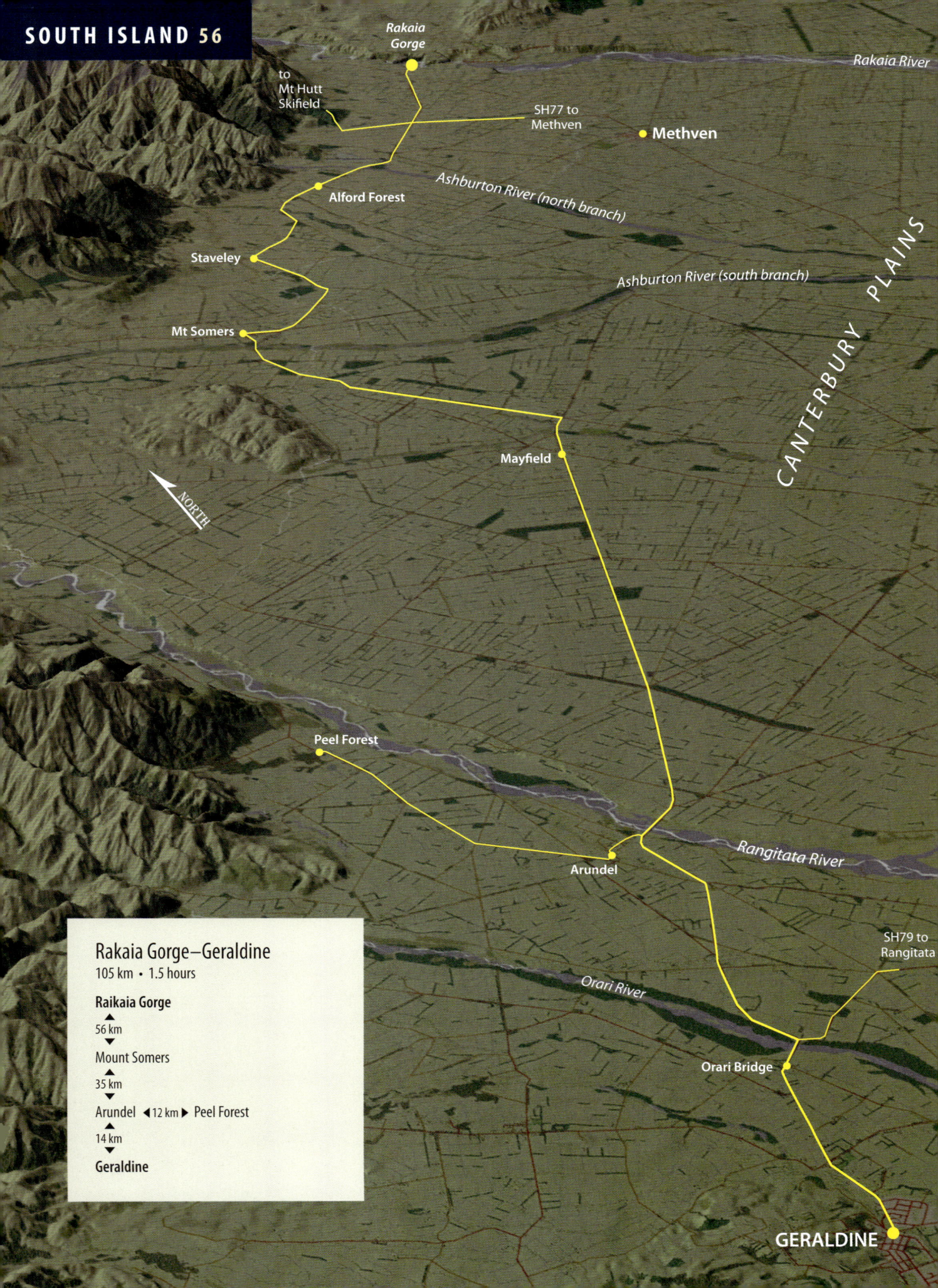

Rakaia Gorge

to Mt Hutt Skifield

SH77 to Methven

Methven

Alford Forest

Ashburton River (north branch)

Ashburton River (south branch)

Staveley

Mt Somers

CANTERBURY PLAINS

NORTH

Mayfield

Peel Forest

Arundel

Rangitata River

SH79 to Rangitata

Rakaia Gorge–Geraldine
105 km • 1.5 hours

Raikaia Gorge
▲
56 km
▼
Mount Somers
▲
35 km
▼
Arundel ◄12 km► Peel Forest
▲
14 km
▼
Geraldine

Orari River

Orari Bridge

GERALDINE

Rakaia River

Rakaia Gorge–Geraldine

Although this stretch can be driven in about 1 hour, there are a number of side trips along the way. The turnoff to Mt Hutt skifield is 7 km from Mt Hutt Station (the skifield road is closed in summer). Methven, a 13-km detour off SH 72, has a good information centre and a number of cafés. Stavely, a little further along SH 72, has a store with snacks, tea and coffee. From here there is access to Mt Somers and several good walks. Follow the signs to Sharplin Falls Scenic Reserve, which has an easy 45-minute (one way) track for viewing Sharplin Falls.

Mount Somers

The Mount Somers Conservation Area features rugged bush, open subalpine tussock lands, historic coalmines, impressive volcanic formations and deep canyons. The first visitors to this area are believed to have been Maori moa hunters 500–800 years ago. Although no permanent sites of occupancy are documented, primitive drawings in rock shelters on Mt Somers/Te Kie Kie are evidence of these early visitors. Coal deposits were discovered by European settlers in 1856, and extraction began shortly afterwards with the construction of a steep railway track up to 760 metres. The coal was low quality lignite and the mine became uneconomic by 1954, when several underground fires resulted in its closure. Relics and dross from this period are still visible on a number of walks in the area.

The premier walking experience here is the Mt Somers Subalpine Walkway, which can be started at either the Sharplin Falls car park or Woolshed Creek car park. Access to Woolshed Creek (camping, toilets, information) is through Mount Somers township. Follow the Ashburton Gorge Road for 10.5 km then turn down the signposted road 3.5 km to Woolshed Creek picnic area. To complete this walk you need to allow one long day, or arrange to stay a night at one of the huts along the route. Walkway highlights include an old coal mine, water caves, lava formations, waterfalls and panoramic views of the high country. There's also a variety of short walks in the area – the 20-minute Nature Trail and 30-minute Miners Track are both rewarding.

Ashburton Lakes – campground

From Mount Somers township the Ashburton Gorge Road follows the South Branch of the Ashburton River to the Hakatere/Ashburton Lakes, an area of wetlands and tussock of national significance. The largest of the lakes is Lake Heron, a nature reserve and wildlife refuge with high numbers of New Zealand scaup. The red tussock communities around Lake Heron are some of the best remaining in Canterbury. Lake Clearwater has a campground with a public toilet, but no other facilities, and is popular with windsurfers, swimmers, fisher folk and canoeists. Lake Clearwater is a smaller lake, and can be walked around in 3–4 hours by people of average fitness, though the swampy area at the western end of the lake requires some care.

Peel Forest

Close to the Rangitata River, about 12 km north of Arundel, is Peel Forest Park, a 700-hectare remnant of the podocarp forest that once covered much of mid-Canterbury, and a popular holiday spot for Cantabrians. Peel Forest still has a wide range of vegetation, from dense virgin stands to exposed herb-field communities. It enjoys a mild moist climate that provides ideal conditions for ferns – 36 per cent of all ferns that grow in New Zealand occur in Peel Forest Park.

Geraldine – campground

Geraldine is a pleasant mid-Canterbury town, and a busy waypoint for those travelling to Mount Cook or further south. There are plenty of tearoom/cafés but for a more relaxed dining experience seek out the Verde Café down the lane opposite the turnoff to Mount Cook. Other Geraldine highlights include specialty chocolates at the Chocolate Brown shop, a vintage car museum and several easy walking trails.

From Geraldine, drive south 11 km to Winchester to rejoin SH 1. If travelling to Mount Cook and the Mackenzie Country, take SH 79 to Fairlie (46 km, 45 minutes) and join SH 8 from Washdyke (see Christchurch–Wanaka, Route 62).

Lake Clearwater

CHRISTCHURCH

CANTERBURY PLAINS

73

Waimakariri River

Kirwee

Darfield

Sheffield

Springfield

Porters Pass

TORLESSE RANGE

73

Lake Lyndon

to Porter Heights Skifield

Castle Hill Village

Cave Stream

to Mt Cheesman Skifield

Flock Hill

to skifields

Purple Hill

CRAIGIEBURN RANGE

Lake Pearson

Cass

Waimakariri River

73 Bealey Spur

Klondyke Corner

Bealey River

ARTHUR'S PASS

to Greymouth

NORTH

Christchurch–Arthur's Pass

160 km • 2.5 hours

Christchurch
▲
48 km
▼
Darfield
▲
24 km
▼
Springfield
▲
36 km
▼
Cave Stream
▲
52 km
▼
Arthur's Pass

57 Christchurch–Arthur's Pass SH 73
160 km, 2.5 hours

This superb route across the Southern Alps over Arthur's Pass was opened in 1866 – an astonishing feat given the rugged terrain early roadbuilders had to contend with, especially on the western approach up the Otira Valley. Even today there is a constant threat of rockfall, and the pass is regularly closed by snow in winter. But the completion of a viaduct from the pass to the Otira River has eased the journey somewhat, and there are continued upgrades planned on the highway's difficult sections.

The most noticeable feature of this drive is the changing landscape as you progress westwards. Beyond the Canterbury Plains the highway climbs to open tussock grasslands beyond Porters Pass, and enters beech forest and high alpine terrain as it nears Arthur's Pass National Park. After the gradual rise through Canterbury's dry high-country landscape, the abrupt plunge toward the West Coast brings a rapid transition to dense rata and podocarp forests on this wetter side of the Alps.

Darfield
Express Yourself café provides good coffee and food but was one of the few cafés I encountered that uses non-biodegradable polystyrene cups. For more substantial meals go to the Terrace Café and Bar.

Springfield and the Canterbury Plains
Springfield (72 km from Christchurch) is the last town before the road climbs to Porters Pass. Springfield's tradition of hospitality dates to when horse-drawn Cobb & Co coaches travelled to and from the West Coast between 1866 and the 1920s. Yello Shack Café is now the best option here.

Porters Pass (945 m) – walks, picnicking
Beyond Springfield the highway approaches the Torlesse Range which features the distinctive square-cut Torlesse Gap – according to local legend, flying through the gap has exercised a few daredevil pilots. The range is within the Torlesse Conservation Park, which protects the area's unique and rare alpine flora and fauna. SH 73 reaches Porters Pass and nearby Lake Lyndon at the southern end of the Torlesse range after a short haul from the plains. In winter this is a popular tobogganing and ski touring spot.

Kura Tawhiti Conservation Area – picnicking, walks
From Porters Pass the road sweeps towards Arthur's Pass along wide glaciated valleys. A few minutes drive from Porters is the turnoff to Porter Heights skifield, and shortly after on the left is Kura Tawhiti Conservation Area – a weird landscape of limestone boulders favoured by rock climbers, botanists and walkers. It is also a place revered by the West Coast's Waitaha tribe. Castle Hill village has no facilities for travellers.

Cave Stream – walks, picnicking
Limestone boulder fields, scarps and vast unbroken scree fields dominate the vistas over the next few kilometres between Castle Hill, Flock Hill and Craigieburn Forest Park. At Cave Stream Scenic Reserve, up the hill from the Mt Cheeseman skifield turnoff, is a 'free caving' experience where in low flows it's possible to scramble through a limestone cave. Take a torch, wear strong shoes, dress for the wet and cold and don't attempt it when the river is high, if it's raining or looking like rain.

Craigieburn Forest Park/Flock Hill – campground, walks, skiing
Beech forests arrive on the landscape at Craigieburn Forest Park where an unserviced camping area is located a few minutes from Cave Stream. Access roads lead to Broken River and Craigieburn skifields, then after a short winding section is Flock Hill Station.

Flock Hill–Bealey – walks
Lake Pearson, home to a rare colony of crested grebe, is squeezed between hillsides and the long shifting screes on Purple Hill. Beyond here the route opens into space again toward Cass and the Waimakariri River. As the road edges past bluffs above the Waimakariri, horizons expand toward the Main Divide peaks, forests and tussock grasslands of Arthur's Pass. Just over Bruce Creek is a collection of holiday baches on Bealey Spur about a kilometre from the Bealey Hotel, where you can ask Paddy to tell you the one about the moa.

Near Castle Hill Village, Waimakariri Basin (Andris Apse)

GREYMOUTH

Grey River (Mawheraui)

6

Kumara Junction

SH6 to
Hokitika

Kumara

73

Moana

Lake Brunner (Moana)

HOHONU RANGE

Jacksons

Taramakau River

Aickens

73

Otira River

Otira

Mt Rolleston

Otira Viaduct

M A I N   D I V I D E   S O U T H E R N   A L P S

Arthur's Pass

Bealey River

73

to Christchurch

NORTH

Arthur's Pass – Greymouth SH 73, 6
93 km, 1.5 hours

Arthur's Pass – walks, skiing

The highway enters the park at the Bealey Bridge over the Waimakariri. Klondyke Corner, the prominent forested corner on the opposite bank, has a camping ground and picnic area. Arthur's Pass village is located in the forested Bealey Valley 160 km from Christchurch. The DoC visitor centre has information and excellent displays on the park's natural and human history. A Cobb & Co coach takes pride of place at the centre, which is a short distance from the railway tunnel (completed in 1923) that ended the era of horse-drawn transport over the pass. Take note also of the displays explaining the challenging construction of the viaduct and cantilevered section of road just west of the pass, before you drive through it. Of the short walks near the village, I would recommend the Devils Punchbowl Track (1.5 hours return).The Wobbly Kea is the pick of the village's cafés.

From the village SH 73 enters the alpine zone as it winds up the pass (920 m). There is a superb lookout up the Bealey Valley. Although Maori have been using the pass for centuries, the memorial near the highpoint is to the explorer Arthur Dudley Dobson who was the first European to cross it, in 1864. The view of Mt Rolleston from the steep Temple Basin skifield track (3 hours return) is one of the best in the park. A more sedate but rewarding short walk can be enjoyed in the Upper Otira Valley which is peppered with alpine flowers in summer. NB: This is an alpine region and walkers should be equipped for mountain weather.

Devil's Punchbowl Falls, Arthur's Pass National Park

Otira Gorge

The descent into the Otira rapidly brings you to a vastly different milieu of huge boulders, rainforest and a dark, foreboding valley which is leavened in summer by bright displays of rata. The painter Petrus van der Velden's bleak representations of the valley in the 1890s (one of which is hung at Christchurch's Robert McDougall Art Gallery) will seem familiar when you've been here in a storm. Below the gorge, Otira settlement is an untidy collection of railways-related buildings and a pub.

From Otira, the highway turns west at Aickens where the Otira River meets the wide and braided Taramakau. Like Springfield, Jacksons Hotel 18 km from Otira, has long been a travellers' rest, and offers whitebait sandwiches, gourmet pies and cosy couches. From Jacksons, Greymouth is 62 km away via Kumara Junction and SH 6, or about 75 km via Moana and Lake Brunner.

Upper Otira Valley

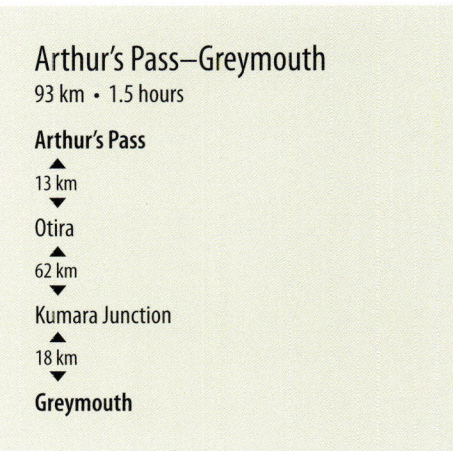

Arthur's Pass–Greymouth
93 km • 1.5 hours

Arthur's Pass
▲
13 km
▼
Otira
▲
62 km
▼
Kumara Junction
▲
18 km
▼
Greymouth

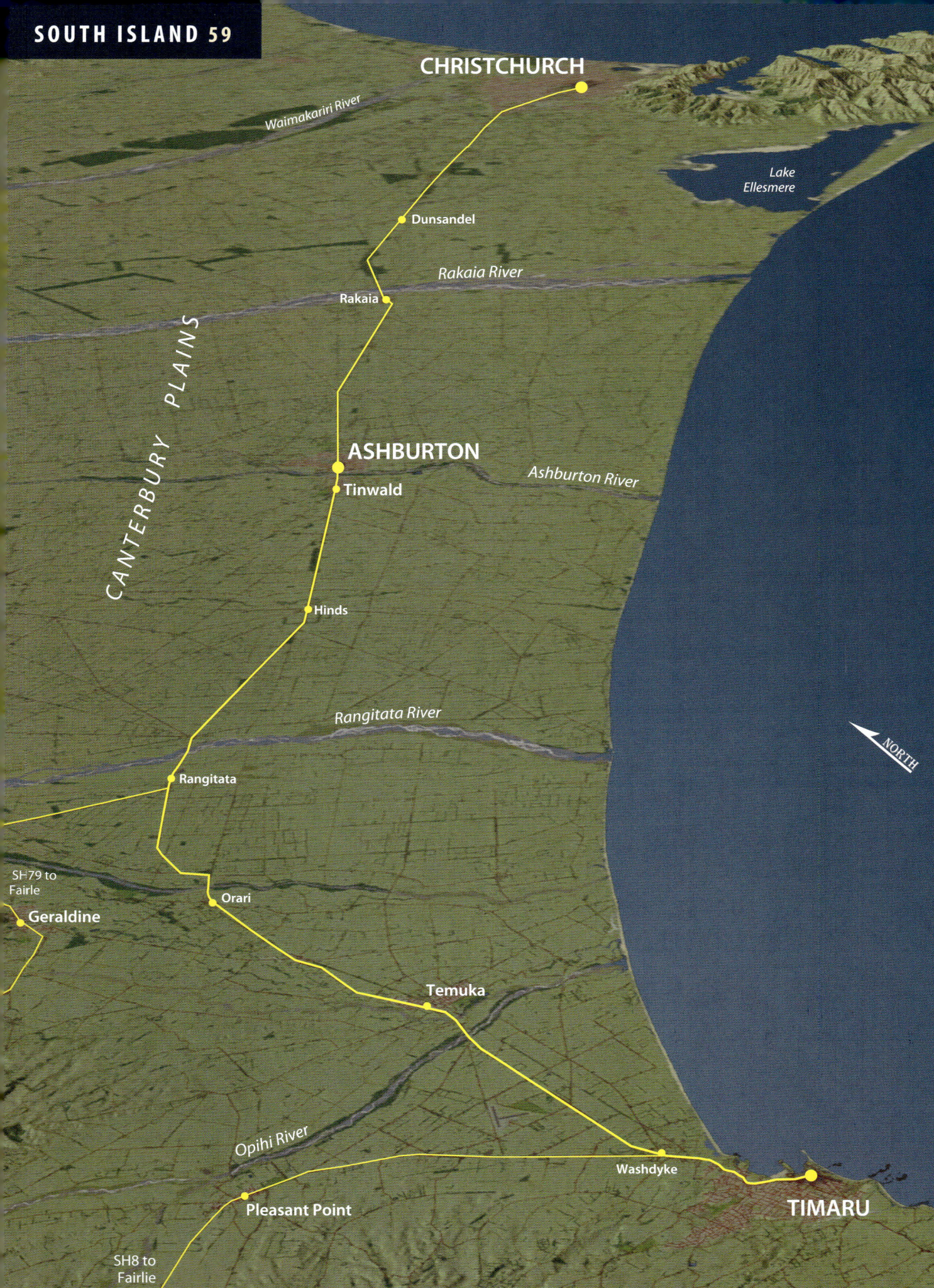

CHRISTCHURCH

Waimakariri River

Lake Ellesmere

Dunsandel

Rakaia River

Rakaia

CANTERBURY PLAINS

ASHBURTON

Tinwald

Ashburton River

Hinds

Rangitata River

NORTH

Rangitata

SH 79 to Fairlie

Geraldine

Orari

Temuka

Opihi River

Washdyke

Pleasant Point

TIMARU

SH8 to Fairlie

59 Christchurch–Timaru SH 1
164 km, 2 hours

The drive south across the Canterbury Plains to Timaru is a necessary chore that must be endured to reach routes to Mount Cook, the Waitaki Valley, Central Otago, Dunedin and further south to the Catlins. Fortunately there are plenty of roadside fruit stalls and dairies for ice-cream stops, as well as a choice of good cafés and good beaches to stop at south of Timaru. Most centres have playgrounds if the kids need to burn off some energy.

Dunsandel/Rakaia
The Dunsandel Store has been converted into a fine travellers' café/delicatessen with good food, coffee, ice-creams, juices and a pleasant courtyard out the back. Continuing south, you cross over New Zealand's longest bridge, spanning the Rakaia River, one of New Zealand's most significant braided rivers. At Rakaia village is the very modern Salmon Tales Café.

Ashburton
Ashburton is about 1 hour from Christchurch. Turn off at Ashburton along SH 77 to reach Methven and Mt Hutt skifield. Ashburton's Botanic Gardens are well worth a visit. For a bite to eat try the Ashford Craft Village café on the bypass around the town, Kelly's Café and Bar on the main street or the Café Time Bakery just beyond the town centre, south of the bridge.

Those intending to drive to Mount Cook can turn off SH 1 at Rangitata onto SH 79 towards Geraldine and Fairlie (see Woodend–Geraldine, Route 56). Alternatively, you can take the longer route along SH 8 from Washdyke, shortly before Timaru (just over 2 hours from Christchurch).

Orari/Temuka
Orari is a small place, but Café Mes Amis beckons travellers. From here there is a slightly more direct route around Geraldine to Fairlie. Temuka is larger and has a nice collection of attractive nineteenth-century buildings. Try the Brix café on the bypass around the main street.

Timaru
Entering Timaru, pass by Motel Row, then turn left into the Piazza where you will find the Blue Bay Café overlooking Caroline Bay. Further on, as you head down Stafford Street, is the Purple Lizard Café. The Aigantighe Art Gallery is one of the country's best regional galleries.

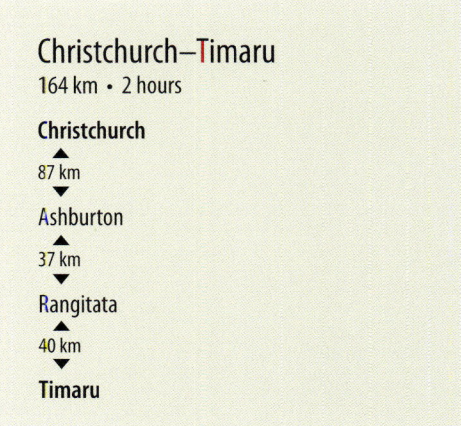

Christchurch–Timaru
164 km • 2 hours

Christchurch
▲
87 km
▼
Ashburton
▲
37 km
▼
Rangitata
▲
40 km
▼
Timaru

Near Timaru

TIMARU

Pareora

Otaio

Hook

Waimate

SH82 to
Kurow

① 1

Glenavy

Waitaki River

SH83 to
Kurow

Pukeuri

OAMARU

Cape Wanbrow

Maheno

Herbert

Moeraki Boulders

KAKANUI MOUNTAINS

Moeraki

Hampden

Katiki

*Katiki
Beach*

Shag Point

SH85 to
Alexandra

① 1

Palmerston

Waikouaiti

Karitane

Seacliff

Warrington

Waitati

① 1

SILVER PEAKS

Otago Harbour

NORTH

Timaru–Dunedin
199 km • 3 hours

Timaru
▲
86 km
▼
Oamaru
▲
43 km
▼
Moeraki
▲
28 km
▼
Waikouaiti
▲
42 km
▼
Dunedin

DUNEDIN

60 Timaru–Dunedin SH 1
199 km, 3 hours

South of Timaru, SH 1 follows coastal plains to the Waitaki River and Oamaru. Just before Hook is the Berry Barn Café, where you can also buy a range of seasonal berries. Thirty minutes from Timaru, just beyond Hook, SH 82 turns to Waimate township and up the north bank of the Waitaki River to Kurow (71 km from SH 1, see Omarama–Oamaru, Route 61).

Oamaru – campground, walks
Oamaru (3 hours from Christchurch) is world-renowned for its well-preserved collection of classical Victorian buildings made of 'Oamaru stone' (also called whitestone, a chalky limestone quarried in the district). In my opinion, this is New Zealand's most significant and impressive historic area, and well worth a visit. The fully-restored Harbour Street Historic Precinct houses several galleries, a pub and other shops. Your jaw will drop on entering the Whisky Store and Café in Harbour Street — explore the barrels full of whisky upstairs, then taste a little at the ground floor counter. At the northern end of town you can visit the Whitestone Cheese Factory and shop on Torridge Street (delicious cheese). For a bite to eat there is the Whisky Store Café, or try Latitude 45 opposite the railway station (corner of Ribble and Humber Streets). Oamaru is the childhood home of the novelist Janet Frame and the setting for many of her early novels — a heritage trail allows walkers to visit sites that feature in those works. This and other trails, including the 'Ocean to Alps' trail up the Waitaki Valley, are covered by the *Heritage Trails of North Otago* booklet (free at information centres). The opportunity to view blue and yellow-eyed penguins returning to their nests at dusk is another outstanding Oamaru attraction. Follow the signs around the harbour to the penguin colony where you will also find the Portside Restaurant with the best ocean views in town.

Moeraki Boulders/Moeraki Village – campground, walks
The remarkable 60-million-year-old Moeraki Boulders are located on Moeraki Beach 43 km south of Oamaru, between Hampden and Moeraki village. The short walk along the beach to the boulders begins from a Department of Conservation carpark signposted off the highway (go straight ahead once you've turned off the highway). There is quicker access from the nearby café, but unless you are a café patron a donation is sought to cross land to reach the beach. The café is a missed opportunity — save your discretionary café dollars for Fleur's Place at Moeraki Village. The 45-minute Millenium Walkway offers a good introduction to the area — once the location of a large Maori settlement.

Shag Point – walks, picnicking, wildlife
The association with Maori along this coast is continued as you drive south over a headland to the beautiful Katiki Beach and Shag Point, once a stronghold of a Ngai Tahu hapu or sub-grouping. The reef off the mouth of the Shag River is said to be the upturned hull of the Arai-te-Uru canoe, one of the great mythical waka that bore Maori's Polynesian ancestors to Aotearoa. A seal colony, sea lions and penguins can be observed from the Shag Point Scenic Reserve on the signposted side road around Shag Point towards the river mouth.

Palmerston/Waikouaiti
A short distance from Shag Point is the village of Palmerston (about 45 minutes before Dunedin). SH 85 – known to locals as 'the Pigroot' (apparently a reference to the number of pigs in the area in settler days) – leads westwards towards Ranfurly (see Route 65). Continuing south to Dunedin, SH 1 traverses hill country to Waikouaiti (Waikouaiti Beach is great), returning to the coast at Waitati (Blueskin Bay), before climbing over Kilmog Hill to Dunedin.

Karitane–Warrington coast route – swimming, views
A shorter, slower but scenic diversion south of Waikouaiti is the coastal drive from Karitane to Warrington. Karitane is a popular beach resort and fishing settlement with a long and interesting history. It was first colonised by Maori and later by whalers, then the South Island's first mission station was established here as settlers established themselves in the nineteenth century. Given this history the small museum at Seacliff is an interesting place to visit.

Moeraki boulders

WAIMATE

SH1 to
Timaru

Pukeuri

OAMARU

Waitaki River

83

Duntroon

Maerewhenua River

Takiroa rock drawings

SH82 to
Waimate

Otekaieke

Hakataramea River

Hakataramea

Kurow

Lake Waitaki

Lake Waitaki

Aviemore

Lake Aviemore

Otematata River

Otematata

Ahuriri Pass

Otamatapaio River

NORTH

Benmore Dam

83

Otamatapaio River

C U T H B E R T   R A N G E

Lake
Benmore

OMARAMA

Omarama–Oamaru
119 km • 1.75 hours

Omarama
▲
24 km
▼
Otematata
▲
29 km
▼
Kurow
▲
23 km
▼
Duntroon ◄24 km► Danseys Pass
▲
43 km
▼
Oamaru

61 Omarama–Oamaru SH 83

119 km, 1.75 hours

The drive down the Waitaki Valley from Omarama is flanked by stark high-country scenery and merino runs, but it's the artificial lakes of the Waitaki hydro scheme that dominate the landscape. The scheme produces one-third of New Zealand's electricity from eight power stations. Three hydro lakes – Benmore, Aviemore and Waitaki are on this route – (the remaining five power stations are in the upper Waitaki). The drive is covered by the 'Ocean to the Alps' heritage trail in the *Heritage Trails of North Otago* booklet (free from information centres).

Otematata/Benmore dam – swimming, fishing, boating

The first lake on the Waitaki is Lake Benmore, the largest of the country's hydro storage lakes, which is retained by one of the largest earth dams in the Southern Hemisphere (built in 1966). To reach Benmore dam turn off at Otematata. A visitor centre at the dam site makes good use of displays to describe the workings of the Waitaki scheme and electricity generation system to the North Island, but suffers from overzealous spin-doctoring about its environmental virtues. From here you can drive across the dam and around the northern shores of Lake Aviemore, returning to SH 83 at Aviemore.

Aviemore and Waitaki dams

The Aviemore dam, 19 km from Otematata, is an earth and concrete structure completed in 1969. Lake Waitaki, smallest of the three hydro lakes, filled the valley after the Waitaki dam was finished in 1934. Opposite the Waitaki dam are 12 stone buildings originally built in 1927 as accommodation for dam construction workers. They are being steadily restored, and one now contains the pleasant Café Hydro.

Kurow – campground

Kurow, with a population of about 411, is the largest centre in the valley. Many of its older buildings are constructed from Oamaru stone (see Oamaru above). From here the Waitaki River flows undammed to the sea: the trout and salmon fishing on the river is reputedly world class. The best option for lunch is the Valley Café and Bakery.

Takiroa Maori Rock Drawings

These well-preserved charcoal and ochre rock drawings are found under a limestone overhang off the highway 3 km from Duntroon. While some drawings were unceremoniously chopped out of the wall and spirited to museums or private collections, the bulk remain. Interpretive panels describe the drawings and their origins.

Duntroon/Lower Waitaki – campground

Nicol's Blacksmith Shop with its working nineteenth-century forge, the Vanished World Museum and Flying Pig Café are worth setting aside time for a stop in Duntroon. Also worth considering is the scenic drive over Danseys Pass to Naseby and Ranfurly (SH 85, see also Dunedin–Cromwell via Middlemarch, Route 65). The route initially follows the Maerewhenua River to the Danseys Pass Holiday Park. Beyond here the road is unsealed, narrow and winding and should be driven carefully, if only to allow an appreciation of the wonderful tussock landscapes and schist outcrops on the pass. Not suitable for campervans. Allow 1.5 hours to Naseby.

Lake Benmore (Andris Apse)

Rangitata River

TIMARU

Washdyke

Orari River

Temuka

Winchester

1

Pleasant Point

to
Rangitata

Geraldine

Opihi River

Cave

*KAKAHU
FOREST*

Tengawai River

Opuha River

Albury

8

79

Pukaki River

Ohau River

Allandale

Fairlie

Opihi River

NORTH

ALBURY RANGE

Kimbell

Burkes Pass

Burkes Pass

Christchurch–Tekapo
222 km • 3.5 hours

Christchurch
▲
133 km
▼
Geraldine
▲
46 km
▼
Fairlie
▲
25 km
▼
Burkes Pass
▲
18 km
▼
Tekapo

— — — — RANGE

8

Tekapo River

Tekapo Canal

LAKE TEKAPO

Lake Tekapo

62 Christchurch–Wanaka SH 1, 79, 8
416 km, 6.5 hours (see maps this page and overleaf)

After climbing to the Mackenzie Basin from the Canterbury Plains, this drive traverses picturesque high country flanking the Southern Alps, past Aoraki/Mount Cook National Park and over Lindis Pass to Wanaka, a base for excursions into Mount Aspiring National Park. The parks, mountain ranges and sequence of large glacial lakes are all part of the Te Wahipounamu South-West New Zealand World Heritage Area.

Christchurch–Tekapo, 222 km, 3.5 hours

From Christchurch take SH 1 south through Rakaia and Ashburton (see also Christchurch–Timaru, Route 59). There are two routes to Fairlie from here. The first and quicker option is to leave SH 1 south of Rangitata and follow SH 79 to Fairlie via Geraldine (see Woodend–Geraldine, Route 56 for notes on Geraldine); the second is to continue to Washdyke and take SH 8.

From Geraldine the route to Fairlie leaves the flatlands and wends its way through farmed hill country to reach a high point overlooking the Opuha Valley (location of the Farm Barn Café) and the Two Thumb Range.

If driving from Washdyke, SH 8 to Fairlie allows easy travel up the Opihi and Tengawai valleys to Pleasant Point where the Pleasant Point steam railway operates in summer. The railway museum at the station doubles as an information centre, and Legends Café across the railway line is recommended.

Fairlie – campground
Marketed as the 'gateway' to the Mackenzie Country, Fairlie's greatest redeeming feature for travellers is the Old Library Café – Eat Deli Café is another good option. Mackenzie was reputedly a wily Scottish drover cum sheep rustler whose legendary exploits led to his name being permanently fixed to the area.

Burkes Pass and the Mackenzie Basin
The actual gateway to the Mackenzie Country is 25 km west of Fairlie at Burkes Pass where SH 8 slips between the Two Thumb and Dalgety ranges. Below the pass on the Fairlie side is Burkes Pass settlement (tearooms). A description of the pass as a 'portal' is very apt, for here SH 8 enters the vast glaciated Mackenzie Basin, a region of lakes and undulating high-country grasslands below the Southern Alps. Shortly beyond the pass is a lookout offering a first view of Aoraki/Mt Cook.

Lake Tekapo – campground, fishing
Tekapo is a holiday destination where scenic flights and the stone Church of the Good Shepherd on the lakeshore are especially popular with tourists. Another big attraction, due to the very clear night sky unpolluted by city light, is the Mt John Observatory. The newest facility is an ice rink and spa complex on the edge of town. Lake Tekapo is the first of three large glacial lakes in the basin, all of which have been harnessed by the Waitaki power scheme (see notes on Omarama–Oamaru, Route 61). Canals traverse the basin linking lakes with power stations, and long lines of pylons take away the energy generated.

Lake Tekapo

Mount Cook Village

BEN OHAU RANGE

Tasman River

Dobson River

Lake Tekapo

LAKE TEKA

8

Tekapo Canal

Lake Pukaki

Lake Pukaki

Pukaki River

Pukaki Canal

TWIZEL

Ohau River

Ohau Canal

Lake Ruataniwha

Lake Ohau

Ohau Skifield

Lake Ohau Village

DIADEM RANGE

8

clay cliffs

SH83
Oama

OMARAMA

Ahuriri River

DUNSTAN RANGE

8

NORTH

Lindis Pass

Tekapo–Lindis Pass, 117 km, 2 hours

The 47-km drive from Tekapo across the Mackenzie Basin past Lake Pukaki to the turnoff to Aoraki/Mount Cook National Park takes 30–40 minutes. Chances are though you'll stop often to appreciate the expansive and arresting lake/grasslands/mountain vistas, even when clouds are pouring over the ranges during a nor'wester. An alternative route to Lake Pukaki (with great views of Aoraki/Mt Cook) is to drive along the Tekapo Canal to the Tekapo B power station on the eastern shore of Lake Pukaki – the canal drive (signposted 'Salmon Farm') begins about 13 km from Tekapo.

Aoraki/Mount Cook National Park – walks

Mount Cook Village is a 55-km (40-minute) drive along the western side of Lake Pukaki and the Tasman Valley. On a fine day this route offers stunning views of the national park's high peaks and glaciers including the country's highest mountain, Aoraki/Mt Cook (3754 m). Lake Pukaki fills the trench that formed when the Tasman Glacier retreated 10,000–13,000 years ago. The lake's level was artificially raised when the outlet was dammed for hydro-generation.

Aoraki/Mount Cook National Park is primarily an alpine climbing area, but there are a number of easy walks for the day visitor. Many of these, like the walks to Sealy Tarns or Blue Lakes on the Tasman Glacier, lead to interesting glacial landforms and fine views. Red Tarns, a steep 40-minute to 1-hour climb (one way), is well worth the effort for outstanding views of Aoraki/Mt Cook and Mt Sefton. Information about the park is available at the park visitor centre. Near the centre is The Old Mountaineers Café, the only competition for the massive Hermitage Hotel's eateries. Rental car drivers should note that the Tasman Valley Road to the Tasman Glacier may be excluded from insurance cover – that said, the road is a straightforward drive as far as the Blue Lakes carpark.

Twizel – fishing

Twizel arose from the plains as a workers' village while the Waitaki power scheme was being constructed. It survives thanks to a steady tourism trade, the winter skiing industry based at the Ohau skifield, and New Zealanders who turned places vacated by redundant hydro workers into weekend holiday homes. Twizel is the base for a recovery programme for the critically endangered black stilt, a wading bird once common throughout New Zealand but now restricted to the braided rivers of the Mackenzie Basin. Guided tours are the only way to visit the black stilt rearing facility and viewing hide. These tours are very popular so book well ahead through the Twizel Information Centre. In the central Twizel shopping area you will find Hunters Café/bar and Shawty's Café (gourmet pizzas), but Poppies Café near the southern entrance to Twizel is probably the pick of the bunch.

Lake Ohau/Clay Cliffs Reserve – walks, picnicking, fishing

From Twizel SH 8 continues south past Lake Ruataniwha. A side road 13 km from Twizel leads to the shores of Lake Ohau (cafe at the lodge) and to the Ohau skifield. Just before the Ahuriri River, prime black stilt habitat, signs indicate the way to the clay cliffs which are located on a side road above the Ahuriri River. Though on private land (pay a small fee into an honesty box), this spectacular example of badland topography – deeply dissected ravines, pinnacles, gullies and sharp ridges eroded from gravels and silt – is protected by covenant, and is open to the public most of the year. Human connections with the cliffs area date to the earliest Polynesians who hunted moa and other birds from camps in the Waitaki Valley. Maori call the area Paritea, meaning white or light coloured cliff. A walking track leads into the heart of the cliffs area.

Omarama – fishing, gliding

Omarama has several tearooms, but the Clay Cliffs Estate Vineyard Café (500 m past Omarama, open from 11 a.m., closed Tuesdays and in winter) offers pleasant outdoor/indoor eating. The next best option is the Wrinkly Ram at the northern entrance to town. Omarama is world renowned for its excellent gliding opportunities. If this is something you have never tried, give it a go – the experience of unpowered flight can't be beaten. Turn east from Omarama to reach SH 1 via the Waitaki Valley (SH 83, see Omarama–Oamaru, Route 61).

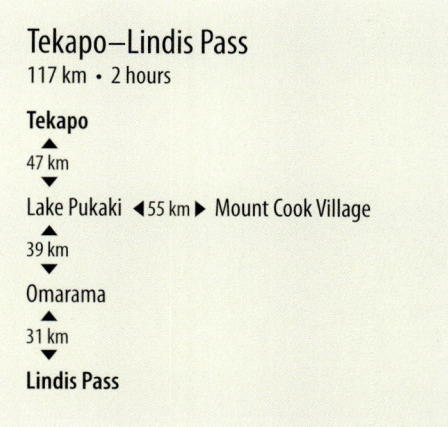

Tekapo–Lindis Pass
117 km · 2 hours

Tekapo
▲
47 km
▼
Lake Pukaki ◀ 55 km ▶ Mount Cook Village
▲
39 km
▼
Omarama
▲
31 km
▼
Lindis Pass

Aoraki/Mt Cook

Lake Hawea

● **Lake Hawea**

Lake Wanaka

Mt Iron

● **Albert Town**

Hawea River

● **WANAKA**

6

Clutha River

● **Luggate**

SH6 to Cromwell

8A

Lindis Pass–Wanaka
77 km · 1 hour

Lindis Pass
▲
47 km
▼
Tarras
▲
21 km
▼
Luggate
▲
9 km
▼
Wanaka

Lindis Pass to Wanaka
77 km, 1 hour

The transition from the Canterbury high country into Central Otago's tawny tussock landscapes is made when SH 8 crosses Lindis Pass (971 m) on the Dunstan Range. Much of the route over the pass occurs within Lindis Pass Scenic Reserve, which protects a large area of red-tussock grasslands. Over Lindis Pass SH 8 descends beside the Lindis River, a tributary of the Clutha. To reach Wanaka turn west on SH 8a just after Tarras (Country Coffee Shop, petrol, toilets).

Wanaka – campground, walks, fishing, skiing, boating

Wanaka is a sublime tourist town on the edge of Lake Wanaka, the fourth largest lake in New Zealand. Drives around its southern shore and up the Matukituki Valley lead to Mount Aspiring National Park with fine views of Mt Aspiring/Tititea. Walks in the Matukituki Valley, and (closer to Wanaka) to lookouts on Roys Peak (6 hours) and Mt Iron (45 minutes) offer spectacular views of the glaciated mountain scenery in this region. Of Wanaka's cafés, Kai Whaka Pai near the lakefront churns out good coffee and cake to the masses, the Ardmore Food Company wins awards, and Relishes has al fresco dining in the summer.

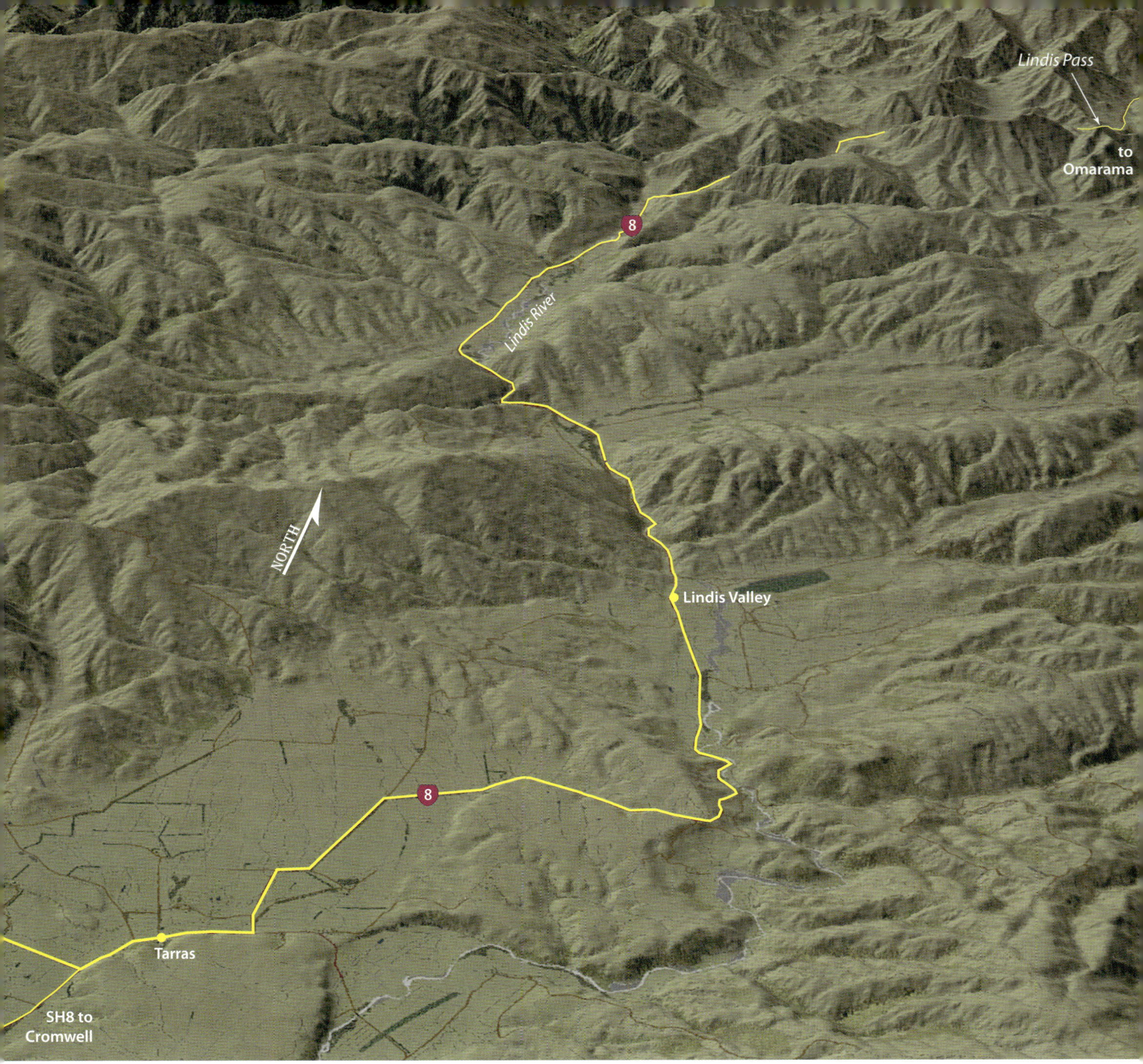
Lindis Pass
to
Omarama
8
Lindis River
NORTH
Lindis Valley
8
Tarras
SH8 to
Cromwell

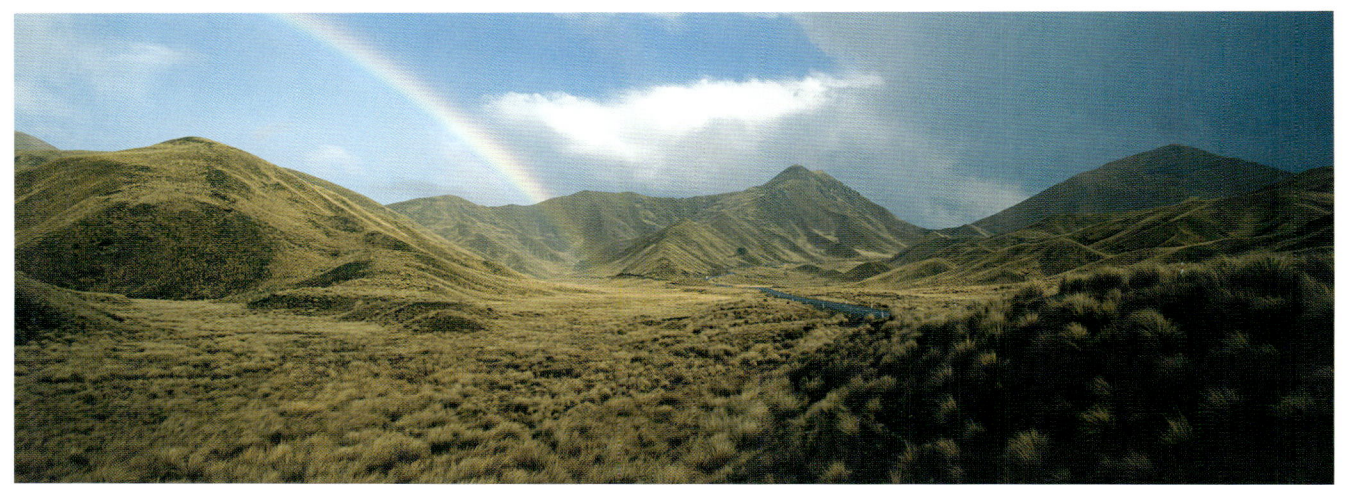

Lindis Pass

Lake Hawea

Lindis River

Lake Wanaka

SH6 to Haast

Clutha River

6

Luggate

WANAKA

Cardrona River

Waiorau Snowfarm

PISA RANGE

Cardrona Skifield

Cardrona

Arrow River

CROWN RANGE

Macetown

Kawarau Gorge

6

Coronet Peak Skifield

Arrowtown

Arrow Junction

Kawarau River

Remarkables Skifield

6

HECTOR MOUNTAINS

Shotover River

THE REMARKABLES

Frankton

Arthurs Point

6A

SH6 to Kingston

QUEENSTOWN

Lake Wakatipu

63 Wanaka–Queenstown

Both routes between these centres have their charms. The SH 6 route takes the traveller through wine- and apricot-growing areas around Cromwell, and then through the Kawarau Gorge past historic mining sites and rugged Central Otago scenery. The Crown Range Road (SH 89) is a scenic alpine route, which reaches the greatest elevation of any public road in New Zealand.

Wanaka–Queenstown SH 6
110 km, 1.5 hours

From Wanaka drive to Cromwell (50 km) along the shores of Lake Dunstan. Close to Cromwell are the Bannockburn and Ripponvale wine-growing areas. Bannockburn's Carrick and Mt Difficulty wineries have good cafés, while in Cromwell try the Fusee Rouge or Tin Goose cafés in the centre of town, or visit the historic area of Old Cromwell down on the lakefront where you will find the Grain and Seed Café.

Kawarau Gorge

12 km from Cromwell at the entrance to the Kawarau Gorge is the Goldfields Mining Centre, a working gold claim where visitors can pan for gold, view mining relics and machinery. Keeping high on its left bank, SH 6 follows the Kawarau River as it flows through the gorge's narrow defile below steep and overhanging walls of layered schist. Beyond the Nevis River confluence the route crosses the Kawarau and follows open terraces where several well-known Central Otago vineyards – including Gibbston Valley and Chard Farm – are located. Where the gorge narrows again is the famous A.J. Hackett Bungy (the world's first commercial bungy operation) off the historic Victoria Bridge. The Crown Range route from Wanaka meets SH 6 at Arrow Junction near Arrowtown.

Arrowtown – campground, walks, picnicking, swimming

Arrowtown is a picturesque holiday village, a short distance from SH 6, and 19 km from Queenstown. The area's colourful goldmining past is recreated at the town's museum, while walks towards Macetown reveal mining relics. There's pleasant swimming and picnicking by the Arrow River. Saffron Restaurant is well known for its food and service. Chocoholics should seek out the Patagonia Chocolate shop.

Crown Range Road SH 89
54 km (to SH 6 at Arrowtown), 1 hour

This scenic traverse of the Crown Range offers a quick route to Queenstown. Sticky date pudding is an opportunity never to be missed so stop at the Fe Café on the way out of town. SH 89 travels south from Wanaka up the Cardrona Valley, past the historic Cardrona Hotel and the Cardrona Skifield. The climb through tussock landscapes to the crest of the Crown Range reaches 1121 metres, with spectacular views of Lake Wakatipu and the area's glacial landforms in the far distance. The descent toward Arrowtown is steep, culminating in a zigzag below Crown Terrace to SH 6.

Approaching Queenstown, newly-built suburbs testify to this region's rapid growth, before the western flank of The Remarkables is revealed. SH 6 turns left at a major roundabout, passes by the airport, crosses the Kawarau River (the only river outlet from Lake Wakatipu), then heads south. Continuing into Queenstown, the road follows the shoreline of Frankton Arm before dipping down to the CBD in Queenstown Bay. Popular cafés include Vudu, Joe's Garage and Halo.

Wanaka–Queenstown
110 km • 1.5 hours

Wanaka ◄ 54 km ► Arrow Junction via Crown Range Rd

▲
50 km
▼

Cromwell

▲
41 km
▼

Arrow Junction

▲
19 km
▼

Queenstown

---

18 to ...narama

DUNSTAN MOUNTAINS

Lake Dunstan

8

...ipponvale

CROMWELL

Alexa...
C...

Bannockburn

NORTH

Lumsden

SH6 to Lumsden

Five Rivers

Mossb
Te A

6

Athol

Garston

Mataura River

HECTOR MOUNTAINS

EYRE MOUNTAINS

Kingston

Halfway Bay

NORTH

Drift Bay

THE REMARKABLES

6

Lake Wakatipu

QUEENSTOWN

to Frankton

to Frankton

64 Queenstown–Milford Sound SH 6, 94
308 km, 5 hours (see maps this page and overleaf)

The 116-km Te Anau–Milford Highway in Fiordland National Park is undoubtedly one of the most rewarding drives in New Zealand. When it's fine the route combines spectacular mountain and forest scenery with some very good short walks and camping areas. In the wet, mountainsides become laced with waterfalls, and while driving may require more care, it is never dull. Fiordland incorporates almost half the 2.6-million-hectare Te Wahipounamu South-West New Zealand World Heritage Area, which recognises the outstanding natural and cultural features of this extraordinary landscape. For most tourists, Milford Sound is the 'must-visit' scenic icon of New Zealand, and because of that you must also put up with the worst aspects of mass tourism – crowds, tour buses, and noisy aircraft.

Queenstown–Te Anau, 2.5–3 hours
To reach Te Anau from Queenstown take SH 6 along the southern arm of Lake Wakatipu, around what's known as 'The Devil's Staircase', past Kingston to Five Rivers. Here you turn off to Mossburn where SH 94 leads across undulating farmland beneath the Takitimu Mountains to Te Anau. The drive around Lake Wakatipu is the most scenic part of this leg, with its views to the Eyre Mountains.

Kingston
There are several lake-edge picnic sites near and at Kingston, home of the Kingston Flyer, a vintage steam train service which puffs its way to Fairlight and back in 90 minutes, departing daily at 10 a.m., 1.30 p.m. and 3.45 p.m. There's a tavern and café at the Kingston Station.

Athol
Were it not for the Lazybones Café, Athol, just under an hour from Queenstown, would be of little interest to travellers. But this is an excellent roadside eatery, and if leaving Queenstown early I'd recommend skipping that expensive Queenstown breakfast and heading straight to Athol to experience fine country cooking and mastery of the espresso machine.

Mossburn
Claiming to be the deer-farming capital of the world, Mossburn also has Bracken Hall, a small gift shop that just happens to make good coffee and cake.

Mavora Lakes – campground, walks, picnicking
The Mavora Lakes Park is 39 km along an easy unsealed road that leaves SH 94 about 12 km from Mossburn. It is a wonderful, beech-forested location, great for swimming, picnicking and fishing.

Beyond the Mavora Lakes' turnoff, SH 94 passes briefly through the Red Tussock Conservation Area, and from near The Key come first views of the Fiordland mountains.

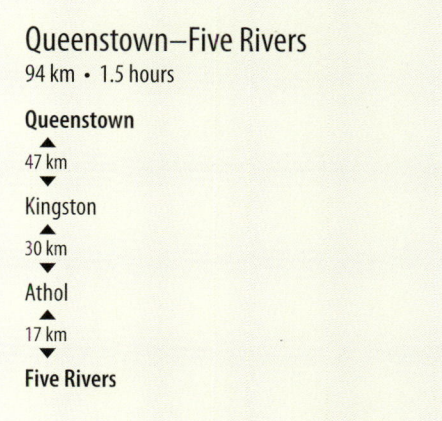

Queenstown–Five Rivers
94 km • 1.5 hours

Queenstown
▲
47 km
▼
Kingston
▲
30 km
▼
Athol
▲
17 km
▼
Five Rivers

TSS Earnslaw on Lake Wakatipu, Queenstown

Mavora Lakes

MURCHISON
MOUNTAINS

Lake Te Anau

Te Anau Down

South Fiord

TE ANAU

94

SNOWDON
FOREST

The Key

Mararoa River

Centre
Hill

EYRE
FOREST

94

Oreti River

Mossburn

SH94 to
Lumsden

NORTH

Five Rivers

SH6 to
Lumsden

The map on the left shows:

Eglinton River

94

Mavora Lakes

EYRE MOUNTAINS

Five Rivers–The Divide
166 km • 2.5 hours

Five Rivers
▲
21 km
▼
Mossburn ◀ 51 km ▶ Mavora Lakes
▲
59 km
▼
Te Anau
▲
86 km
▼
The Divide

to Queenstown

Parawa

6

Mataura River

Te Anau – campground, walks, picnicking

On the south-eastern shores of Lake Te Anau, this township is a very busy tourist centre in the summer months. The Fiordland National Park visitor centre is located near the eastern outskirts of the town, close to the DoC-run Te Anau Wildlife Centre where a number of native bird species can be viewed in aviaries. Among them are takahe, a critically endangered species whose only wild population is across Lake Te Anau in the Murchison Mountains. DoC's *Fiordland National Park Day Walks* brochure has good information on the natural features, short walks, campsites and other aspects of the Milford Highway and greater Fiordland area. The Olive Tree Sandfly Café down The Lane next to the Fiordland Cinema is my pick of the local cafés, with Redcliff Restaurant/Café the happening place in the evening (often with live music).

Milford Highway

The highway to Milford Sound is just as impressive as the sound itself, but it would be a mistake to do the drive and not take a cruise. The busiest cruises occur around the middle of the day – in summer dozens of coaches drive from Queenstown to meet them, so to avoid choking on diesel fumes book a cruise for earlier or later in the day, or better yet, overnight in Te Anau. Without stopping you can reach Milford Sound in about 2 hours, but you'd be missing plenty. The sandflies are savage – repellent is a must for walkers and campers. Buy fuel at Te Anau – the return journey is within the range of most vehicles though fuel can be purchased (at great cost) at Milford or Gunn's Camp. In winter, the road may be closed by avalanches or snow.

The first leg of the journey to Milford is alongside Lake Te Anau, with views early on across the lake up the South Fiord and to the Stuart and Murchison mountains. Milford Track walkers need drive no further than Te Anau Downs, 30 minutes from Te Anau. From here the highway shifts inland past recovering stands of forest to the darker red beech forests of the Eglinton Valley.

Mackay Creek – campsites, walks, views, picnicking

The open grassy expanses of the river flats at Mackay Creek offer the first significant view of Fiordland's dramatic landscapes, which like the rest of the Southern Alps were carved by vast glaciers. What's different is that the erosion-resistant qualities of Fiordland's granite, gneiss and diorite rocks have preserved the glacial imprint in its steep walls, summits and U-shaped valleys – when elsewhere in the South Island softer rocks have given way to a less angular topography.

Mirror Lakes – campsites, walks, views

A 5-minute boardwalk excursion to a valley-edge wetland, with clear pools containing trout and waterfowl (including scaup, mallard and shags). Forest birds flit through red and silver beech forest, from common tomtits and fantails to the rare rifleman.

Knobs Flat – shelter, campsite

A public shelter here has panels describing the road's history, the work of avalanche controllers, natural history and the world heritage area.

Lake Gunn

The 45-minute Lake Gunn nature walk (76 km from Te Anau) is accessible to wheelchairs.

The Divide–Milford Sound

48 km • 1 hour

The Divide ◀ 12 km ▶ Hollyford
▲
30 km
▼
Homer Tunnel
▲
18 km
▼
Milford Sound

The Cha
Cleddau River

WICK MOUNTAINS

Milford
Track

EARL MOUNTAINS

Knobs Flat

Lake Te Anau

Eglinton River

94

LIVINGSTON

Mirror Lakes

Mackay Creek

Anau

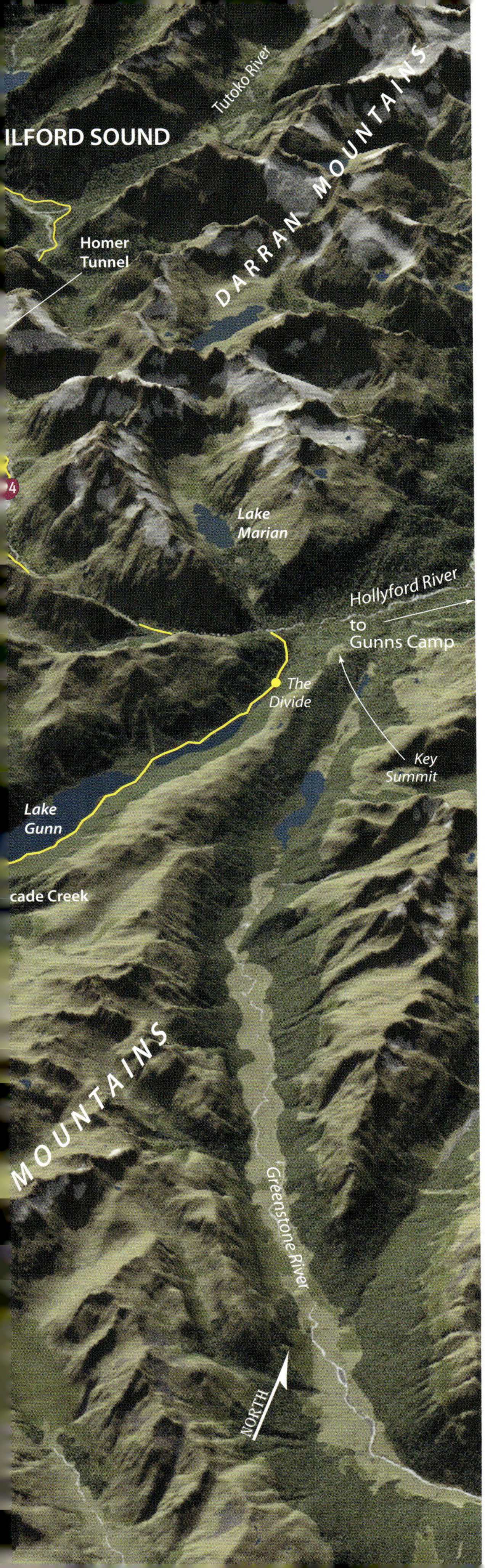

The Divide – shelter, walks

The Divide is the forest pass separating the Eglinton and Hollyford valleys. It is the start and finish point for the Routeburn and Greenstone tracks, as well as the popular walk to Key Summit (3 hours return), a subalpine wetland offering outstanding views of Fiordland and north towards Mount Aspiring National Park. From the Divide, SH 94 enters the most spectacular section of the highway, beginning with the steep descent to the Hollyford River. Pops View is a well-situated lookout with vistas east to the Humboldt Mountains, and west towards the U-shaped hanging valley of Marian Creek below Mt Crosscut.

Hollyford Valley – campground, walks

The Hollyford Road (unsealed) branches off northwards at the base of the descent. A 10-minute forest walk along the Lake Marian track, about a kilometre from the junction, crosses the Hollyford to reach a spectacular cataract. Gunn's Camp, 8 km from the junction, features a campground, store, a great little museum, and the droll humour of camp-owner Mr Murray Gunn.

From the junction SH 94 climbs the steep fall of the Hollyford River to the subalpine grass and shrublands of the upper Hollyford Valley. Near the Homer Tunnel, the prominent pyramid of Mt Talbot overlooks boulder fields and vegetation decimated by winter and spring avalanches. On the right, up the Gertrude Valley, is the aptly named Mt Barrier.

Homer Tunnel/Cleddau Valley – walks

Homer Tunnel, constructed between 1934 and 1954, bores through Homer Saddle to the Cleddau Valley. At the carpark at the Hollyford end you'll quite likely encounter inquisitive kea, a mountain parrot, but please observe the entreaty not to feed them. At the tunnel's western end the road emerges into the breathtaking Cleddau Valley and starts a winding descent to the Cleddau River. In a storm the sight of waterfalls cascading thousands of metres down the bluffs is unforgettable.

The short walk to The Chasm takes you to where the Cleddau River is forced through a slot gorge. As you descend through forests toward Milford Sound there are occasional sightings of snowcapped Mt Tutoko (2746 m), the highest peak in Fiordland – best viewed from the Tutoko River bridge. Just past the Donne River are first views of Mitre Peak.

Milford Sound – campground, walks, boat cruises

It's not possible for the overexposure of Mitre Peak and Milford Sound in countless brochures, posters and tourist department advertisements to take anything away from your first sight of them. Milford is busy and noisy, but if you can stay longer than an hour, you'll find a moment of quiet and perhaps some solitude on a walk to appreciate how wonderful the place is.

The only place for lunch or a meal is the Blue Duck Bar and Café. Accommodation options are few – a backpacker hostel and campground located a kilometre back up the road, or an overnight cruise.

65 Cromwell–Dunedin via Middlemarch SH 8, 85, 87
266 km, 3.5 hours (see maps this page and overleaf)

This route traverses Central Otago where wide undulating valleys float between dun-coloured ranges – landscapes turned mythical by *The Lord of the Rings* films, painter Grahame Sydney and the makers of car and beer ads.

Clyde/Alexandra – campground
From Cromwell it's a 20-minute drive around Lake Dunstan to Clyde and Alexandra. Clyde has shaken its recent hydro-town past and reverted to sleepy holidaysville with several travellers' cafés (try the Post Office Café) and old stone buildings made straight out of the schist landscape. All of which neatly complements nearby Alexandra's wine and historical trails and roadside stalls selling the stone fruits for which the area is famous. Alexandra has an interesting museum and gallery located inside the information centre building.

Omakau/Ophir
The Muddy Creek Café in Omakau is okay (rabbit and bacon pie anyone?). Turn right at Omakau to explore the nearby tiny village of Ophir, for which a brochure is available. For fine views of the Central Otago landscape, continue 4 km toward Poolburn to the crest of the Ragged Ridge.

Saint Bathans – walks, picnicking, swimming
SH 85 continues up the Manuherikia Valley alongside sheep runs and localities with little more than a pub to their name. Historic Saint Bathans, 17 km off the highway (sealed) from Becks, is one of the best preserved sites in the Otago Goldfields Park. The town's collection of nineteenth-century wooden, stone and mud-brick buildings stands on the edge of disused goldworkings that date to the 1860s gold rush. The rustic mudbrick Vulcan Hotel (1882) is still open for business, serving meals and drinks.

Ranfurly/Naseby – walks, biking, panning, campground
From Becks, SH 85 rounds Ragged Ridge and North Rough Ridge and enters the expansive tussock grasslands of the Maniototo Plain beneath the Hawkdun Range. Ranfurly has reinvented itself as a centre for rural art deco and has an interesting railway station museum and the E-Central Café. Naseby, 14 km north of Ranfurly, is a lovely village with period buildings, craft shops, a village green and Black Forest Café. The historic Danseys Pass Hotel and Kyeburn Gold Diggings is 20 minutes from Naseby along a rough unsealed road. (Allow 45 minutes to reach Palmerston and SH 1 from Ranfurly.)

Middlemarch–Mosgiel
Just past Kyeburn turn south onto SH 87 for the 129-km/1.5-hour drive through Middlemarch to Mosgiel and Dunedin. Flanked by the Rock and Pillar Range, SH 87 follows the meandering Taieri River and the justly popular Central Otago Rail Trail – an old railway route developed into a walking track and mountain bike trail. At Hyde you will find the Otago Central Hotel and Café serving rail

trail bikers and anyone else that happens along. Beyond Middlemarch (Kissing Gate Café) the highway climbs through rolling hills, offering fine views back towards the Maniototo before it descends to Outram (good coffee at Wobbly Goat Café) and Mosgiel to join SH 1.

66 Queenstown–Dunedin via Clutha Valley SH 8
290 km, 4.5 hours (see map overleaf)

Queenstown to Alexandra (94 km) is a scenic 1.5-hour drive through the Kawarau Gorge to Cromwell and along the shores of Lake Dunstan (this leg of the route is described in the Wanaka–Queenstown, Route 63 and Cromwell–Dunedin, Route 65 sections).

From Alexandra, SH 8 travels south down the Clutha Valley, renowned for its orchards, brown trout and quinnat salmon fishing, and jet boating on the Clutha River. Between Alexandra and Roxburgh the route tracks through a distinctive Central Otago landscape, flanked on the west by the Old Man Range and on the east by the Knobby Range. There are expansive views over the Clutha, undulating grasslands and outcrops of schist. You can sample this landscape on the 40-minute interpreted walk at the Flat Top Hill Conservation Area 6 km from Alexandra. It's worth having the *Clutha District Heritage Trail* brochure on hand if you're interested in the area's gold mining past.

Roxburgh – campground
Lake Roxburgh was formed when the Clutha was dammed near Roxburgh in the early 1950s – at one stage this was the largest dam in New Zealand (the largest now is Benmore in the Waitaki Valley). Award-winning Succulents Café is located in Roxburgh township, 40 km from Alexandra, the centre of the valley's pip-fruit growing industry. Also in Roxburgh is the smaller Caffeine Café, making a nice roast vege salad. Tours of Roxburgh's orchards and gardens are a popular activity and there is a museum situated in a former Methodist Church (1872). The Lake Roxburgh walkway offers another opportunity to stretch your legs.

Roxburgh–Lawrence
SH 8 continues southwards through Ettrick and Millers Flat (dairy, campground, pub). At Raes Junction, 72 km from Alexandra, SH 90 turns off to Gore (67 km – gallery and café at Tapanui). A little further down the road, SH 8 crosses the Clutha at the historic Beaumont Bridge (1887). Next to the bridge is the start of the Millenium Track, which wanders down the Clutha's east bank.

Lawrence
Lawrence etched its place in New Zealand history when gold was struck in nearby Gabriel's Gully in May 1861 – a discovery that helped lift New Zealand out of economic depression and brought 10,000 diggers to the area. Gabriel's Gully is a short drive from Lawrence, with interpreted walking tracks and a great picnic spot. Lawrence has several cafés providing good personal service, including the Lemon Tree (the only café in New Zealand to spell 'panino' correctly as the singular of 'panini'). SH 1 is joined 37 km from Lawrence, just south of Milton, and 50 minutes (61 km) drive from Dunedin.

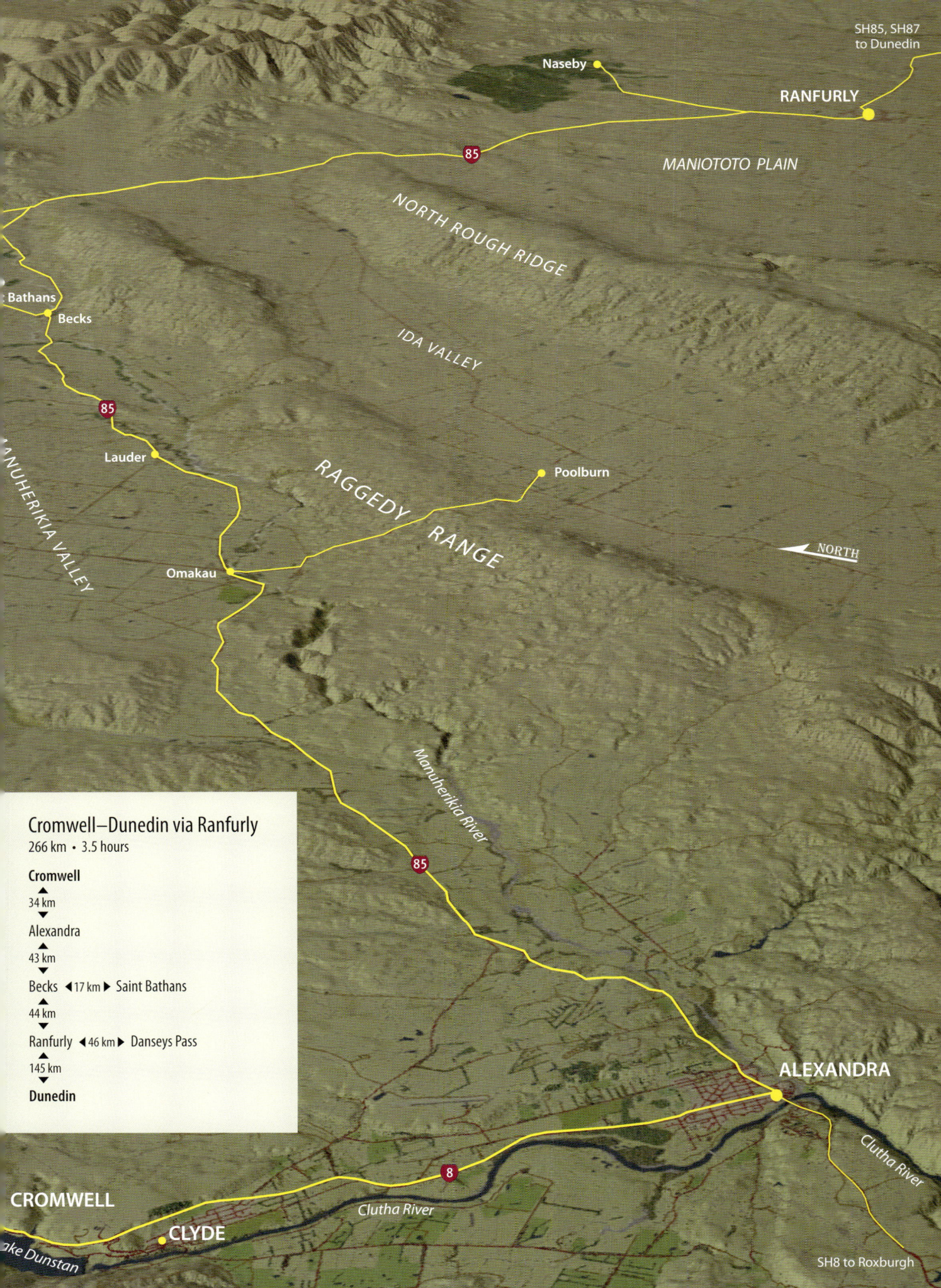

SH85, SH87
to Dunedin

Naseby

RANFURLY

85

MANIOTOTO PLAIN

NORTH ROUGH RIDGE

: Bathans

Becks

IDA VALLEY

85

Lauder

Poolburn

RAGGEDY RANGE

← NORTH

Omakau

Manuherikia River

85

Cromwell–Dunedin via Ranfurly
266 km • 3.5 hours

Cromwell
▲
34 km
▼
Alexandra
▲
43 km
▼
Becks ◄ 17 km ► Saint Bathans
▲
44 km
▼
Ranfurly ◄ 46 km ► Danseys Pass
▲
145 km
▼
Dunedin

ALEXANDRA

Clutha River

Manuherikia River

Clutha River

CROMWELL

8

CLYDE

ke Dunstan

SH8 to Roxburgh

to Queenstown

ALEXANDRA

KNOBBY RANGE

OLD MAN RANGE

Lake Roxburgh

Roxburgh

8

Ettrick

Millers Flat

Clutha River

Lake Onslow

LAMMERMOOR RANGE

LAMMERLAW RANGE

SH90 Raes Junction

Beaumont

Gabriels Gully

Lawrence

Waitahuna

Lake Mahinerangi

8

BERWICK FOREST

Lake Waihola

Waiho

Milton

SH1 to Balclutha

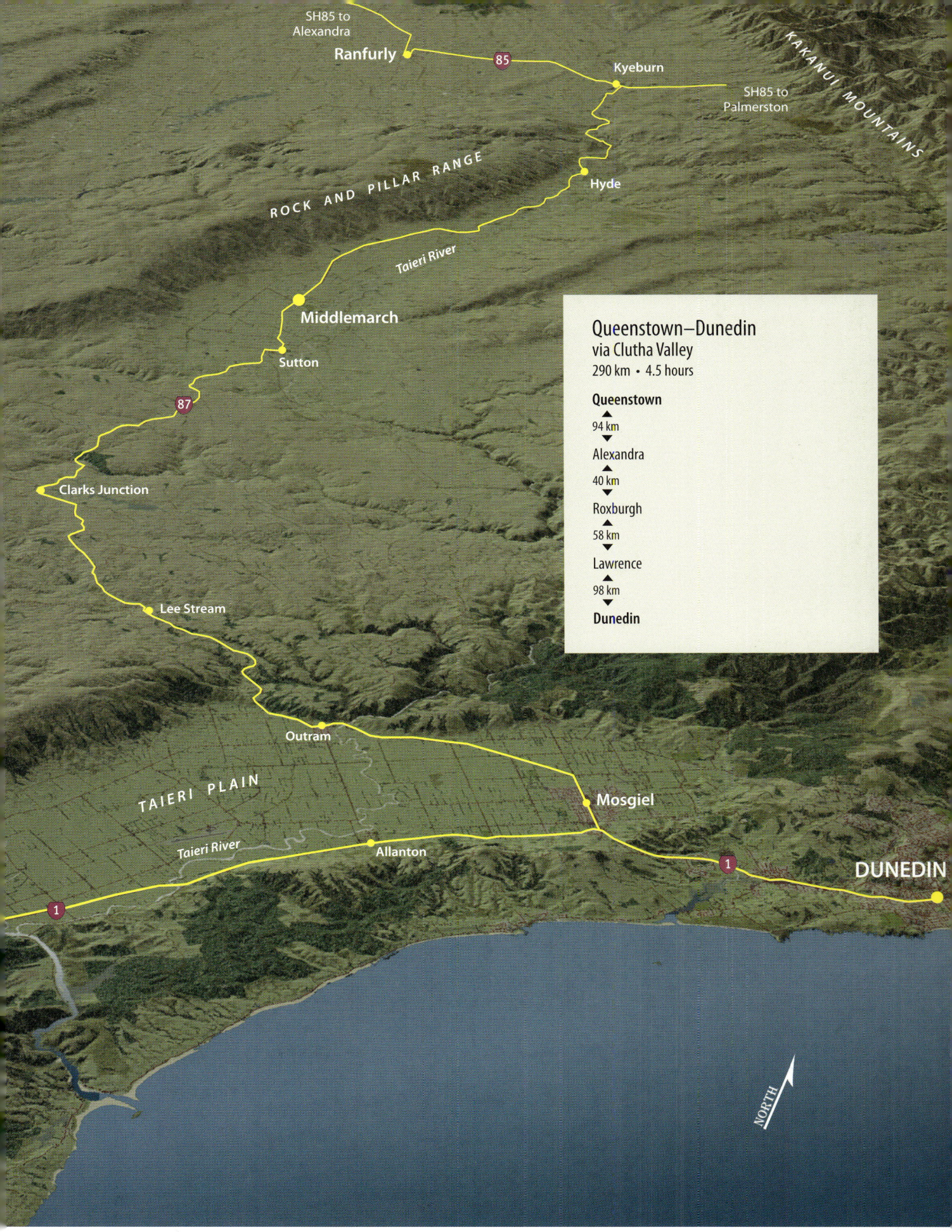

SH85 to
Alexandra

Ranfurly 85

Kyeburn

SH85 to
Palmerston

KAKANUI MOUNTAINS

Hyde

ROCK AND PILLAR RANGE

Taieri River

Middlemarch

Sutton

87

Clarks Junction

Lee Stream

Outram

TAIERI PLAIN

Mosgiel

Taieri River

Allanton

1

DUNEDIN

1

NORTH

Queenstown–Dunedin
via Clutha Valley
290 km • 4.5 hours

Queenstown
▲
94 km
▼
Alexandra
▲
40 km
▼
Roxburgh
▲
58 km
▼
Lawrence
▲
98 km
▼
Dunedin

Dunedin–Invercargill
219 km • 3 hours

Dunedin
▲
41 km
▼
Waihola
▲
41 km
▼
Balclutha
▲
31 km
▼
Clinton
40 km
▼
Gore ◀18 km▶ Mandeville
▲
66 km
▼
Invercargill ◀30 km▶ Bluff

LAMMERLAW RANGE

SH90 to
Tapanui

Clir

1

93

94

Mandeville

Gore

*HOKONUI
HILLS*

Mataura

SH96 to
Winton

● Wyndham

Edendale

1

Dacre

SH98

Mataura River

1

AWARUA PLAINS

● **INVERCARGILL**

1

to
Bluff

Map labels

Otago
Peninsula

DUNEDIN

Waldronville

Brighton

Taieri Mouth

Waihola

ICK FOREST

Milton

Balclutha

Clutha River

Waipapa Point

etoes Bay

NORTH

67 Dunedin–Invercargill SH 1

219 km, 3 hours

Dunedin–Taieri Mouth–Lake Waihola

The quickest route from Dunedin to Invercargill is by SH 1 across the Taieri Plains, but there's a worthwhile coastal variation that follows the Southern Scenic Route along the coast south of Dunedin as far as Taieri Mouth. Look for the Southern Scenic Route turnoff from SH 1 south of the city centre and make for Waldronville. Black Head is an impressive basalt cliff east of Waldronville – well worth the few extra minutes required to divert there. The route passes the beach resort of Brighton (store) and follows the beautiful sandy coastline to Taieri Mouth. Here it turns inland to Lake Waihola (unsealed for 12 km, excellent views) where it rejoins SH 1. Walks up to 4 hours can be made in the Taieri River gorge. Camping and picnicking sites are located at Taieri Mouth and Brighton. Lake Waihola is a popular recreation area, and birdwatchers will enjoy a visit to the Sinclair Wetlands near here.

Balclutha – campground

From Balclutha (try The Gate café), SH 1 heads west toward Clinton and Gore through the rolling country landscape made prosperous by Southland's wool-growers. The stretch between Clinton and Gore was declared the 'Presidential Highway' when President Clinton visited New Zealand in 1999. From Clinton, SH 93 offers a bypass to Mataura (1 hour).

Gore – campground

Gore is a pleasant town on the banks of the Mataura River, a renowned brown trout fishery. The modern, well-designed Hokonui Moonshine Museum and information centre is a must-stop attraction that recounts Gore's colourful history as the centre of an illicit trade moonshining whisky during the area's 'dry' years. Over the road, Gore's innovative Eastern Southland Gallery houses New Zealand's only permanent collection of paintings by Ralph Hotere; it also has an extraordinary collection of paintings – including works by Rita Angus and Theo Schoon and indigenous art from African, Aboriginal and pre-Colombian societies – donated to the gallery by John Money. Ten minutes from Gore on SH 94, Croydon Air Services welcomes casual visitors to its vintage aircraft restoration workshop at Mandeville Airfield – Tiger Moths are a speciality, as are joyride flights. An aircraft museum is now being planned for the site. The adjacent café is a good one, and so is the Howl at the Moon café back in town.

From Gore, Invercargill is about 40 minutes via Mataura and Edendale – both towns feature a large dairy factory. Invercargill has the El Tigre Café, recently declared the best café in the Southland region.

Bluff is 20 minutes south of Invercargill and famous for what some consider to be the most delicious and succulent oysters in the world. A ferry leaves for Stewart Island several times each day from Bluff. SH 1, having started at Cape Reinga at the very northern point of the North Island, ends here at Stirling Point.

Otara

Haldane Bay

Slope Point

Curio Bay

Haldane

Porpoise Bay

Niagara

Waikawa

Chaslands

MACLENNAN RANGE

Makati (Chaslands Mistake)

Waipati Beach

Tahakopa River

BERESFORD RANGE

Tautuku Bay

Papatowai

Maclennan

Tahakopa Bay

Purakaunui Falls

RATA RANGE

Long Point

Catlins River

Purakaunui Bay

Catlins Lake

Owaka

Pounawea

Glenomaru

Ahuriri Flat

Nugget Point

Kaka Point

Willsher Bay

Molyneaux Bay

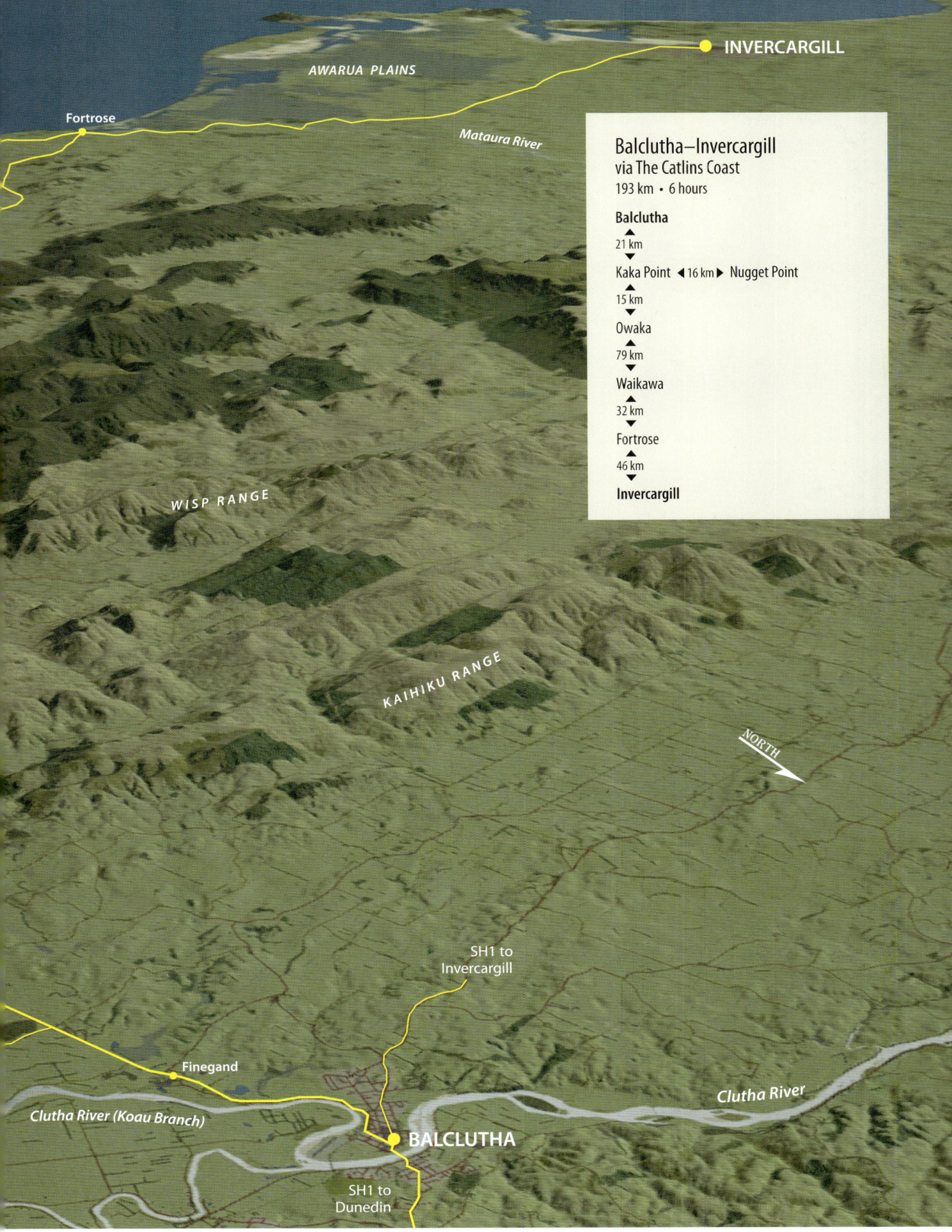

INVERCARGILL

AWARUA PLAINS

Fortrose

Mataura River

Balclutha–Invercargill
via The Catlins Coast
193 km • 6 hours

Balclutha
▲
21 km
▼
Kaka Point ◄ 16 km ► Nugget Point
▲
15 km
▼
Owaka
▲
79 km
▼
Waikawa
▲
32 km
▼
Fortrose
▲
46 km
▼
Invercargill

WISP RANGE

KAIHIKU RANGE

NORTH

SH1 to
Invercargill

Finegand

Clutha River

Clutha River (Koau Branch)

BALCLUTHA

SH1 to
Dunedin

68 Balclutha–Invercargill via the Catlins Coast SH 92
193 km (approximately), 6 hours (see map previous page)

The southeast corner of the South Island is a remarkably beautiful area renowned for its coastal forests, wildlife, beaches and scenery. Mercifully, the Catlins hasn't been subjected to excessive tourism development. What services exist for tourists – the campgrounds, backpackers, homestays and specialist 'eco-tourism' operations are small-scale and low impact, and this feels right for the area. Tourists and providers of small-scale accommodation cottoned on to the potential of the Catlins long before local tourism planners – so much so that the Southern Scenic Route, the premiere touring route through the Catlins, only recently became fully tarsealed. A few side routes to the coast and link roads remain unsealed. Even more bizarrely, the official route bypasses some of the Catlins' most scenic locations. This being the case it requires map-reading and careful driving on a few gravel roads to experience the best from a visit here.

Kaka Point/Nugget Point – campground, walks, views, swimming, patrolled beach
From Balclutha drive south on SH 92 and take the turnoff 6 km from Balclutha to Kaka Point village (15 km from turnoff) on the edge of Molyneux Bay where there is a pleasant beach, store, The Point Café and a kids' playground. From here it's an increasingly spectacular 16-km drive around the coast to Nugget Point. Nugget Point Lighthouse, built in 1869, is an airy but quite safe five-minute walk from the carpark. Fur and elephant seals, New Zealand sea lions, and blue and yellow-eyed penguins are often resident here. Back toward Kaka Point a track leads to the Roaring Bay penguin viewing hides, best used at dusk when penguins are coming ashore.

Owaka, Pounawea and Surat Bay – campground, walks, swimming
To reach Owaka from Kaka Point, take the gravel road from Willsher Bay to SH 92 at Ahuriri Flat. Cannibal Bay Beach (signposted) is a wild beach 8 km from the main road. Owaka (15 km from Kaka Point) is the largest settlement in the Catlins with most services tourists require, including an information centre.

To get to Pounawea, Jacks Blowhole and Surat Bay (on the shores of the Catlins River estuary) turn east at Owaka. There's a campground and safe swimming at Pounawea, while at Surat Bay near the Catlins Heads, New Zealand sea lions are often encountered lounging on the inner beach during summer (while rarely known to have a go at humans, it still pays to give them a wide berth). The beach walk from Surat Bay backpacker lodge to the outer coast is a highlight, particularly when the sea lions are about. Jacks Blowhole is reached after a 20-minute walk across farmland (trail markers, slightly uphill), best viewed at high tide with an onshore wind.

Purakaunui Falls/Purakaunui Bay – campground, walks, picnicking
Just past Catlins Lake (the head of the Catlins River estuary), leave SH 92 again and take the signposted road to Purakaunui Falls. The tarmac soon ends as the road winds toward the remnant beech forest containing the track to the falls (20 minutes return). Before the falls a road leads to Purakaunui Bay where there is a lovely beach with camping and picnicking areas. If you decide to bypass the falls, the main road to Tahakopa Bay crosses Gibbs Hill and the forested Table Hill Scenic reserve (look out for the Matai Falls short walk, 30 minutes return).

Tahakopa Bay/Papatowai – campground, walks, picnicking
From the Purakaunui Falls carpark, take the left fork and continue along the unsealed route to Maclennan on the edge of the Catlins Coastal Rainforest Park. At the bridge over the forest fringed estuary formed by the Tahakopa River is a carpark and the start of the 'Old Coach Road' walk. This is an easy forest walk (40 minutes return) to the river mouth and Tahakopa Bay beach, the site of an early Polynesian moa-hunter camp.

Over the bridge, Papatowai is a small holiday settlement with a pleasant beach-side picnicking spot beneath the totara trees at Picnic Point (kids playground nearby on Mirren Street), and opportunity for long beach walks. On Cross Street (up the hill from the beach access) is the 35-minute Picnic Point forest walk. Blair Somerville's Lost Gypsy Gallery never fails to entertain with his collection of curious creations, devices, gadgets and gizmos. Papatowai once supported a considerable Maori population in pre-European times – from the bones that have been unearthed here it's thought this was one of the last moa habitats in New Zealand.

Tautuku Bay – walks, swimming
Be wary of truckies and others who travel this road at speed. From Papatowai there's a 2-km climb up Florence Hill to the wonderful viewpoint overlooking Tautuku Beach, Tautuku Peninsula and forest from the coast to the Maclennan Range – welcome respite from the sparseness of the farmed landscape encountered on much of the drive thus far. The turnoff to Tautuku Beach is not far down the hill. As well as the beach there are two quality walks from the road worth considering: Lake Wilkie, a 20-minute forest walk; and the Tautuku estuary boardwalk (also 20 minutes).

Cathedral Caves/McLean Falls – walks

Beyond Tautuku Bay, the road crosses a forested range in the Tautuku Scenic Reserve in which rimu, kamahi and roadside groves of fuchsia are striking features. Twelve kilometres from Papatowai is the access to Cathedral Caves at Waipati Beach. The access track crosses private land and is opened only when tides allow. There is a small charge ($5 in 2008) to help maintain the private road, well worth it for the 25-minute walk down a well-made track to the beach and these beautiful limestone caves. Ask at information centres for access and tide details.

At the turnoff to McLean Falls is the very new and welcome Whistling Frog Café and McLean Falls Holiday Park. The café offers a tasty-looking menu including Texel and Highland beef from the associated farm, and local beers. The falls are reached after a 10-minute drive and 15-minute gentle uphill walk (one way).

Waikawa/Curio Bay – campground, walks, swimming

After Chaslands the road passes through a long stretch of native forest, and reaches a T-junction that offers the choice of continuing west along the Southern Scenic Route to Invercargill (80 km), or the more interesting option of heading south to Waikawa, Curio Bay and the coastal route to Fortrose. Towards Waikawa, not far from the junction, is the Niagara Falls Café and Gallery.

Waikawa, 6 km from the junction, has an interesting information centre, museum and great fish and chips from the Blue Cod Blues caravan. Curio Bay, the settlement on the shores of Porpoise Bay, is famous for its surf beach, rare Hector's dolphins, yellow-eyed and blue penguins, seals and the nearby fossil forest.

Seeing the 20 or so Hector's dolphins resident in Porpoise Bay is a delight but there is increasing concern about the impact of tourism on them. Being inshore feeders they will often be seen in the surf – this is the only place in the country where dolphins venture so close in. Given the small size of the group here, and because the species overall is so perilously close to extinction, humans must make a special effort not to disturb these creatures. Indeed, guidebooks promoting the bay as a place to swim with dolphins have caused much alarm. DoC's guidelines stipulate that Hector's dolphins shouldn't be fed, touched or approached (they will move toward you if they want to). Lastly, don't enter the water within 50 metres of a dolphin.

The 180-million-year-old fossilised forest exposed on the outgoing tide at Curio Bay is another of the area's internationally significant marvels. This is part of one of the largest and least-disturbed Jurassic-era fossil forests in the world – stumps, entire trunks and root systems can be discerned in the rock platform and cliffs. The story of the forest is recounted on the information panel at the bay. Unfortunately too many people are venturing into the nearby penguin area and disturbing the easily-spooked birds as they come ashore in the evenings. Tourists are now being asked to not go down to the forest area after 5 p.m.

Slope Point – walk

From Curio Bay the travel is on unsealed roads for approximately 13 km towards Otara. Below another large remnant of forest, the route skirts a dune lake and the tidal estuary inland of Haldane Bay, and eventually reaches a T-junction at Haldane. From here you can make a brief 5-km diversion toward Slope Point, the most southerly point of the South Island. Even if you don't make the 10-minute walk across farmland to the Point (closed in September and October) the drive offers fine views of the coast, Foveaux Strait and Stewart Island. Another vantage point for fine ocean views is at Waipapa Point (turn off at Otara) where lighthouse-spotters can notch up another score. The Southern Scenic Route is joined again at Fortrose (café, fuel), 46 km from Invercargill. As you follow the road beside the Mataura River, notice the tiny private huts guarding fiercely protected whitebait-netting spots.

Purakaunui Falls

Manapouri Power Station

Borland
Lodge

TE ANAU

*Lake
Manapouri*

Manapouri

*TAKITIMU
MOUNTAINS*

*Lake
Monowai*

Blackmount

*Lake
Hauroko*

Lill Burn

Ohai

**ROWALLAN
FOREST**

Clifden

SH96 to
Ohai

96

Aparima Riv

Tuatapere

Waiau River

Te Waewae Bay

LONGWOOD RANGE

Otautau

Orepuki

Monkey Island

99

Pahia Point

Colac Bay

Riverton

Centre Island

NORTH

Te Anau–Invercargill
177 km • 3 hours

Te Anau
▲
22 km
▼
Manapouri
▲
30 km
▼
Blackmount ◄10 km► Lake Monowai
▲
28 km
▼
Clifden ◄34 km► Lake Hauroko
▲
11 km
▼
Tuatapere
▲
48 km
▼
Riverton
▲
38 km
▼
Invercargill

Oreti River

INVERCARGILL

69 **Te Anau–Invercargill via Tuatapere SH 95, 99**
177 km, 3 hours

This route (the western leg of Southland's Southern Scenic Route) follows the forested eastern edge of Fiordland down the Waiau Valley to Te Wae Wae Bay. Scenic highlights are the beautiful glacier-formed lakes: Manapouri, Monowai and Hauroko.

Manapouri – campground, walks, swimming, fishing
Manapouri, 22 km from Te Anau on the edge of Lake Manapouri, is part tourist centre, hydro village and holiday home location. Although its lake, forest and mountain scenery is no less stunning than Te Anau, Manapouri has the virtue of being a far quieter place. Most come here to make the lake cruise to the Manapouri Power Station and the spectacular tour from the station over Wilmot Pass to Deep Cove in Doubtful Sound. Café 23 has given new life to an old church in the village. Nearby Frazers Beach is a good spot for a picnic with tables and a public toilet.

Lake Monowai – campground, picnicking, fishing
The next leg follows the Waiau River as it meanders between Fiordland National Park and the Takitimu Mountains. Lake Monowai is accessed from Borland Road approximately 30 km from Manapouri. The lake is 10 km from the intersection along an easy unsealed road (NB: driving beyond Borland Lodge is not recommended as the road is narrow and poorly maintained). A flat 15-minute walk takes you to a lovely spot with a benchseat overlooking the lake.

Lake Hauroko – campground, picnicking, swimming, fishing
Back on the Southern Scenic Route, continue down the Waiau Valley 28 km to Clifden, site of a beautiful suspension bridge over the Waiau, opened in 1899. The 34-km side trip up the Lill Burn to Lake Hauroko begins 500 metres from the bridge. The road is unsealed but in good condition; the last few kilometres to the lake is through forest. A short forest loop in the Big Totara Reserve leads to a huge 1000-year-old totara.

Tuatapere – campground
Tuatapere, 11 km from Clifden, is the base for exploring the western reaches of the Te Wae Wae Bay coast, Rowallan Forest and multi-day tramps around Fiordland's south coast and the Hump Ridge. Gallery 65 is definitely worth a stop to appreciate the incredible paintings of Fiordland landscapes by a local artist. Yesteryear's Café (and something of a museum) is the pick of slim café pickings.

Te Wae Wae Bay–Riverton – beaches, walks, swimming, campground
Ten kilometres from Tuatapere, SH 99 reaches the magnificent Te Wae Wae Bay. Between here and Riverton are several places of interest, notably McCrackens Rest (views of the bay, information on the area's natural, Maori and European history); Monkey Island, at the eastern end of the bay (sacred to Maori, site of a gold rush tent town, safe swimming, picnicking); Cosy Nook (a delightful fishing settlement); and Colac Bay (excellent beach and campground). Lastly, there's Riverton's superbly located Beachfront Café (turn right before the Aparima River bridge and follow signs to Riverton Rocks), or alternatively the Thyme Out Tearooms (turn up Lex Street from the Riverton Rocks waterfront) for refreshments or a meal.

There are several scenic walks in this area – details from Riverton's information centre on the eastern side of the bridge. The free *Riverton–Aparima South Coast Heritage Trail* brochure provides a useful history of the area. Just after the information centre is the Fiordland Gift Studio with paua (abalone) shell turned into 101 beautiful things, and Mrs Clark's Café.

From Riverton, allow 25 minutes to cross the Aparima and Oreti River floodplains to Invercargill.